EXPLORE *the* BIBLE

ADULT COMMENTARY

Ezra, Nehemiah, Esther

Bob Dunston

Winter 2006-2007

Volume 11, Number 2

D0279324

LifeWay.
CHURCH RESOURCES
Biblical Solutions for Life

ADULT COMMENTARY

This periodical is designed for all adults using the Explore the Bible Series

PRODUCTION & MINISTRY TEAM

Janice Meier
Editor in Chief

David O. Briscoe
Biblical and Instructional Specialist

Jim Frazier
Graphic Designer

Pat Phillips
Copy Editor

Nancy Arnold
Technical Specialist

John McClendon
Lead Adult Ministry Specialist

Mic Morrow, Morlee Maynard
Adult Ministry Specialists

Send questions/comments to
Editor, *ETB: Adult Commentary*
One LifeWay Plaza
Nashville, TN 37234-0175
Or make comments on the Web at
www.lifeway.com

MANAGEMENT PERSONNEL

Ron Brown, Larry Dry
Managing Directors, Leadership and Adult Publishing

David Francis
Director, Sunday School

BILL CRAIG
DIRECTOR, LEADERSHIP AND ADULT MINISTRY

Gary H. Hauk
Director, Publishing
LifeWay Church Resources

ABOUT THE COVER:
Relief of guard from east gate of palace at Susa
ILLUSTRATOR PHOTO/BRITISH MUSEUM 31/15/61

www.lifeway.com
ministry·living·shopping

Printed in the United States of America

Explore the Bible: Adult Commentary (ISSN 0164-4440) is published quarterly by LifeWay Christian Resources of the Southern Baptist Convention, One LifeWay Plaza, Nashville, TN 37234, Thom S. Rainer, President. © 2006, LifeWay Christian Resources of the Southern Baptist Convention.

For ordering or inquiries visit www.lifeway.com, or write LifeWay Church Resources Customer Service, One LifeWay Plaza, Nashville, TN 37234-0113. For subscriptions or subscription address changes e-mail subscribe@lifeway.com, fax 615.251.5818, or write to the above address. For bulk shipments mailed quarterly to one address, e-mail orderentry@lifeway.com, fax 615.251.5933 or write to the above address.

We believe the Bible has God for its author; salvation for its end; and truth, without any mixture of error, for its matter and that all Scripture is totally true and trustworthy. The 2000 statement of *The Baptist Faith and Message* is our doctrinal guideline.

Unless otherwise indicated, all Scripture quotations are taken from the Holman Christian Standard Bible®, Copyright © 1999, 2000, 2002, 2003 by Holman Bible Publishers. Used by permission. Holman Christian Standard Bible®, Holman CSB®, and HCSB® are federally registered trademarks of Holman Bible Publishers.

The suggestions in this resource for pronouncing Bible names are from *That's Easy for You to Say: Your Quick Guide to Pronouncing Bible Names* by W. Murray Severance, © Copyright 1997 by Broadman & Holman Publishers. Used by permission.

ADULT COMMENTARY

IN THIS ISSUE...

EZRA, NEHEMIAH, ESTHER: SEEING GOD'S HAND AT WORK 6

UNIT 1   GOD WORKS THROUGH BLESSINGS
Week of

December   3   **Seizing New Opportunities** 10
Ezra 1:1–3:13

December   10   **Working with Confidence in God**.................................20
Ezra 4:1–6:22

December   17   **Following Godly Spiritual Leaders** 30
Ezra 7:1–10:44

December   24   **Honoring the Savior's Birth***..40
Matthew 1:18–2:12

UNIT 2   GOD WORKS THROUGH COMMITTED INDIVIDUALS
Week of

December   31   **Working Cooperatively**..50
Nehemiah 1:1–3:32

January   7   **Devising Strategies**...60
Nehemiah 4:1–7:73

January   14   **Rededicating Lives**..70
Nehemiah 8:1–10:39

January   21   **Valuing Every Life****..80
Psalms 139:1-24

January   28   **Keeping Commitments**...90
Nehemiah 11:1–13:31

UNIT 3   GOD WORKS THROUGH TURMOIL
Week of

February   4   **When Life Turns Upside Down**....................................100
Esther 1:1–2:23

February   11   **When Service Is Risky**..110
Esther 3:1–4:17

February   18   **How Courage Triumphs** 120
Esther 5:1–7:10

February   25   **What Is Worth Celebrating** 130
Esther 8:1–10:3

*Christmas and Evangelistic Lesson
**Sanctity of Human Life Lesson

INTRODUCING

EZRA, NEHEMIAH, ESTHER: SEEING GOD'S HAND AT WORK

"Look what I did!" can be a frightening exclamation coming from a pre-schooler. She may have dressed herself or tried to give herself a haircut. He may have picked up his toys or drawn on the walls.

"Look what I did!" can also be a frightening expression coming from a believer. It may signal that we are placing undue focus on our own efforts. We rejoice when our obedient service has blessed others, but we cannot take credit for everything we do in life as individuals or as communities of believers. God actively guides us, nurtures our faith, and uses us to accomplish His will. On a regular basis we need to recognize God's hand at work in our lives and thank Him. As you begin this series of lessons, ask yourself the following questions:

How has God worked in my life and how is He working in me today?

How has God worked in my church in the past and how is He working in my church now?

How has God worked in the world in history and how is He working in the world currently?

Historical Background

The events recorded in the Books of Ezra, Nehemiah, and Esther occurred during the time of the Persian Empire. Cyrus the Great (ruled 559-530 B.C.) founded the Persian Empire by defeating the Medes. He then conquered Babylon in 539 B.C. bringing the Babylonian Empire, including Syria and biblical Palestine, under his control and creating a huge empire. Cyrus followed a generous policy toward subject nations. He allowed the Jews in exile to return to Judah and rebuild the temple, taking with them the temple vessels the Babylonians had confiscated when they conquered Jerusalem and destroyed the temple.

Cyrus's son Cambyses II [kam BIGH seez] (ruled 530-522 B.C.) expanded the empire by conquering Egypt in 525 B.C. Darius I [duh RIGH uhs](ruled 522-486 B.C.) brought the Persian Empire to its height of power and influence and extended the borders to include the area from modern-day Pakistan to the Sudan. He continued the generous policies of Cyrus and under his rule the Jews completed the rebuilding of the Jerusalem temple.

Ahasuerus [uh haz yoo EHR uhs](ruled 486-465 B.C.), also called Xerxes I [ZUHRK seez], spent the first part of his reign crushing rebellions in Egypt and Babylon. After experiencing initial success in a campaign against Greece, a series of defeats forced him to withdraw. After Ahasuerus removed Vashti [VASH tigh] as his queen, Esther became queen of Persia, and the Lord worked through her to save His people from destruction.

Artaxerxes I [ahr tuh ZUHRK seez] (ruled 464-424 B.C.) became king following his father Ahasuerus's assassination. In 460 B.C. Egypt, supported by the Athenians, rebelled. Years of fighting finally resulted in a peace treaty with Greece and the regaining of complete control over Egypt in 448 B.C. Judah's proximity to Egypt led Artaxerxes to work hard to create a satisfied, loyal community at the western edge of his empire. Artaxerxes sent Ezra and Nehemiah to Jerusalem to rebuild and reform the community based on God's law.

Alexander the Great conquered Persia in 331 B.C. bringing the once great empire to an end. During the approximately two hundred years of Persian rule, most people believed only the decisions of Persian kings determined their lot in life, but God's work through Ezra, Nehemiah, and Esther demonstrated His hand at work among the Jews and in the world.

Ezra, Nehemiah, and Esther

Ezra traced his lineage through the high priest Zadok back to Aaron, Moses' brother and the first high priest (Ezra 7:1-5). Although from a priestly line, Ezra served as a scribe, one skilled in the interpretation of God's law (7:6). Ezra's name constituted a shortened form of the name Azariah, meaning "the Lord has helped." Artaxerxes I sent Ezra to Jerusalem in 458 B.C., providing him with gifts to support maintenance of and worship in the temple and authorizing him to appoint judges and enforce God's law throughout Judah (7:13-26).

When Ezra arrived in Jerusalem with approximately five thousand other Jews, he dealt with the problem of Jews who had married people of other religions (9:1–10:44). In 445 B.C. following Nehemiah's arrival in Jerusalem, Ezra read God's law to the people, sparking a confession of sin and renewal of the covenant (Neh. 8:1–10:39). Ezra also joined Nehemiah in dedicating Jerusalem's rebuilt wall (12:27-43). God's hand worked through Ezra, calling His people back to obedience.

Nehemiah served as the cupbearer of Artaxerxes I, a highly trusted position since the cupbearer tasted the king's food and drink and thus protected the king's life. Nehemiah's name means "the Lord comforts." When Nehemiah learned of Jerusalem's and Judah's physical and spiritual condition, he asked Artaxerxes to send him to Jerusalem to help rebuild the city walls (Neh. 1:1–2:10). Despite external and internal opposition, Nehemiah led the people in rebuilding the walls and fortifying the city. Nehemiah served as governor for 12 years before returning to Artaxerxes. Sometime later, Nehemiah received Artaxerxes's permission to return, and at that time Nehemiah led the people in a variety of reforms including ceasing work on the Sabbath and dealing with Jewish marriages to non-Jews (13:6-31). God's hand worked through Nehemiah in strengthening Jerusalem's defenses and the people's faith.

Esther was a Jewish orphan, raised by her cousin Mordecai. She rose to become queen of Persia. She lived during the reign of the Persian King Ahasuerus [uh haz yoo EHR uhs], which was prior to the time of Ezra's and Nehemiah's returns to Jerusalem. Esther's Hebrew name *Hadassah* means "myrtle." The name *Esther* is derived from a Persian word meaning "star." The name also has similarities with a Hebrew verb meaning "conceal." Since Mordecai wanted to hide Esther's Jewish identity (Esth. 2:10,20), he may have given her the name *Esther* to help her blend in and to conceal her religious background. After Ahasuerus deposed Queen Vashti, a kingdom-wide search resulted in Esther's becoming queen. When Haman planned to annihilate the Jews, Esther used her position and Ahasuerus's love for her to save her people and defeat their enemies. God's hand worked through Esther to preserve His people.

Authorship

Ezra and Nehemiah comprised one book in the ancient Hebrew and Greek texts. Since the books share a close connection with 1 and 2 Chronicles, many Bible students surmise the same inspired writer, possibly Ezra, wrote all four books. The writer of Ezra and Nehemiah used a variety of source materials including Ezra's memoirs (Ezra 7–10: Neh. 8–10), Nehemiah's memoirs (Neh. 1–7: 11–13), Jewish lists (for example, Ezra 10:18-43; Neh. 7:8-69), and Persian decrees and records (for example, Ezra 1:2-4; 7:12-26). The books probably were written by 400 B.C.

An unknown inspired writer composed the Book of Esther. Some Bible students believe the book was written during the time of the Greek Empire, but in recent times Bible students have argued for an earlier date. The book indicates no Greek influence and the details regarding Persian customs indicate the book was written close to the events described. Probably the book was completed not later than 350 B.C.

Teachings

The Books of Ezra and Nehemiah emphasize five lessons still important for us. First, even though only a relatively small group of Jews lived in Judah and Jerusalem, God continued to work with them by sending Ezra and Nehemiah to provide needed leadership and hope to His people who faced discouragement and difficulty. God continues to provide His people with individuals who supply leadership and vision. Second, the ministries of Ezra and Nehemiah emphasized the importance of the Jews' not allowing their faith to be compromised by non-Jewish ideas and relationships.

While we need to be in the world sharing our faith, we do not need to allow worldly ideas to weaken our faith and witness. Third, the books underscore the centrality of Scripture as a guide to knowing and obeying God. As Ezra led the Jews in studying and living according to God's law, so believers need to study God's Word and apply it daily. Fourth, Ezra and Nehemiah emphasized the importance of worship. We also need to place priority on worship. Finally, the books indicate the importance of prayer. As Ezra and Nehemiah prayed with regularity and faith, we need to do so as well.

The Book of Esther provides four lessons. First, although the book never mentions God, it demonstrates God's continual activity in the world. God worked through Esther and Mordecai to save His people. Even when we have difficulty seeing God at work today, we can rest assured He is actively involved in our world. Second, Esther and Mordecai provide excellent examples of courage and faith for believers today seeking to obey God. Third, the book emphasizes the horror of anti-Semitism and condemns any attempt to exterminate any ethnic or religious group. Fourth, the book emphasizes the importance of remembering and celebrating God's hand at work in the world. As you study Ezra, Nehemiah, and Esther, look for God's hand at work in 5th-century B.C. Persia and consider how God is at work in our 21st-century world. Through the experiences of these three faithful individuals, we can learn to recognize God's hand at work and follow Him.

ADULT EXPLORE THE BIBLE SERIES STUDY PLAN*

	FALL	WINTER	SPRING	SUMMER
2006-2007	Hebrews (Grow Up in Christ!)	Ezra, Nehemiah, Esther (Seeing God's Hand at Work)	1 and 2 Peter (Certainties in Uncertain Times)	Minor Prophets (Majoring on What Matters)
2007-2008**	Matthew (Answers to Important Questions)	Genesis 1–27 (Foundations for Understanding Life's Meaning)	Genesis 28–50 (Foundations for Faith)	Acts (Going into the World)

* Each Fall quarter this chart will be updated to reveal an additional year of the study plan.

**A new eight-year cycle through the Bible begins in Fall 2007. More information will be included in the Spring quarterly.

The Week of December 3

SEIZING NEW OPPORTUNITIES

Background Passage: Ezra 1:1–3:13
Lesson Passages: Ezra 1:1-6; 3:1-3,10-11

INTRODUCTION

"Pastor, during the announcements this morning you mentioned the need for Sunday School teachers. I have not really taught before and am a little nervous about taking on the responsibility, but I am willing to try. I think I would like to work with young adults."

"I'm delighted to hear that Tony," responded his pastor. "We have been hoping to expand our work with young adults by offering additional classes. I appreciate your willingness to help. I am sure we can find someone who can provide guidance and encouragement."

"We certainly can, Pastor, and here I am," exclaimed Jonathan who had been passing by. "Tony, I teach one of the young adult classes. Let's set up a time this week to meet together. We can talk about the Sunday School program and the needs of our young adults, and I'll show you how I prepare a lesson. I would love for you to be part of my class for the next month. You can meet some of our young adults and gain some experience in teaching before you start your own class."

"That is exactly what I need," replied Tony. "When can we meet?"

Most pastors and church leaders would love to hear a conversation like this! Every church has places of service in present, new, or expanding ministries and every Christian can receive a blessing by serving God. Sometimes we let opportunities pass because we feel too overwhelmed by other responsibilities such as caring for children or elderly parents or establishing a business. Sometimes a lack of training or the fear of failure prevents us from serving God. Like Tony we may need a Jonathan who can provide guidance and encouragement.

Seizing opportunities for serving God does not mean we do anything and everything we are asked to do. To serve through the church to the neglect of other God-given responsibilities such as family does not please God. On the other hand, God expects us to take advantage of new opportunities He gives us to participate in His work. We each have a place of service and we need to ask God to help us recognize and seize those opportunities as they come.

Ezra 1:1–3:13

1. Release of the Exiles (Ezra 1:1-11)
2. Resettlement in Judah (Ezra 2:1-70)
3. Rebuilding of the Temple Begun (Ezra 3:1-13)

THE BACKGROUND

In 539 B.C. the army of the Persian King Cyrus attacked and conquered Babylon. With the fall of the city, the Babylonian or Chaldean Empire ended. The Jews in Babylon probably rejoiced. The empire that had conquered Judah, destroyed Jerusalem in 587 B.C., and deported the nation's inhabitants lay destroyed. As the Jews celebrated the destruction of their enemy, they also must have wondered how King Cyrus would rule them.

In contrast to the Babylonian policies, Cyrus respected the customs and religions of his subjects. He ordered the rebuilding of temples the Babylonians had destroyed, the return of treasures taken from the temples by the Babylonians, and the financing of the rebuilding from Persian funds. Cyrus also allowed exiles in Babylon to return to their native lands.

The Jews benefited from Cyrus's policies. In 538 B.C. Cyrus issued a decree allowing Jews to return to Jerusalem to rebuild their temple and nation. He encouraged Jews who wished to remain in Babylon to provide gifts to help the Jews who returned in their rebuilding. Cyrus apparently appointed Sheshbazzar [shesh BAZ uhr] governor of Judah and commissioned him to lead the return (Ezra 1:1-11).

The whole assembly that returned to Judah numbered 42,360, excluding their slaves and singers. The number included individuals from the tribes of Judah, Benjamin, and Levi, and some who could not conclusively establish their ancestry. Upon arriving in Jerusalem, the people assembled at the site of the destroyed temple and gave a generous offering for the rebuilding of the temple and the reestablishing of worship befitting God. The people then settled in the towns where their ancestors had lived (Ezra 2:1-70).

In the seventh month of 537 B.C. the Jews rebuilt the temple altar, celebrated the Festival of Booths, and reinstituted regular sacrifices to God. That same month work began to rebuild the temple. When the people completed the foundation in the second month of 536 B.C., they joined together to praise God for His steadfast love. While most joined in the praise, some wept because they realized the rebuilt temple would not be as magnificent as the temple Solomon had built for the Lord. Joy overcame sorrow as the people celebrated the new beginning God had given them (Ezra 3:1-13).

FOR FURTHER STUDY

What opportunities do you think God is making available for your church to serve Him in your area?

THE BIBLE PASSAGE

1. Release of the Exiles (Ezra 1:1-11)

Verse 1: **In the first year of Cyrus king of Persia, the word of the LORD spoken through Jeremiah was fulfilled. The LORD put it into the mind of King Cyrus to issue a proclamation throughout his entire kingdom and ⌊to put it⌋ in writing:**

In 559 B.C. Cyrus became king of Anshan in Persia (modern-day southern Iran). He served under the control of his grandfather Astyages, who ruled Media (generally modern-day northern Iraq and Iran). Early in Cyrus's life Astyages had dreamed Cyrus would someday supplant him as king and had sought to kill him but failed. Cyrus rose to power in Persia and, after strengthening his army, attacked and conquered his grandfather.

Cyrus then took control of Sardis in Lydia (the western part of modern-day Turkey) in 546 B.C. and turned his attention to Babylon. In October 539 B.C. Babylon fell to Cyrus, and Cyrus became ruler of a huge empire. The **first year of Cyrus** probably referred to 538 B.C., the first full year of his reign as ruler of all Mesopotamia, including Babylon.

The phrase **the word of the LORD spoken through Jeremiah** referred to several passages in Jeremiah. First, Jeremiah prophesied Babylonian domination for 70 years followed by Judah's restoration (Jer. 25:11-12; 29:10). Bible students have suggested several ways to count the 70 years. Some count the years beginning with the fall of Nineveh to the Babylonians in 612 B.C. until the fall of Babylon in 539 B.C. Others count from the beginning of Nebuchadnezzar's reign in 605 B.C. to Cyrus's conquest in 539 B.C. Still others believe Jeremiah referred to the time between the temple's destruction in 587 B.C. to the completion of its rebuilding in 516 B.C. Although none of the suggestions results in an exact 70 years, all three suggestions have merit, produce a number rounded off to 70, and indicate the accuracy of Jeremiah's prophecy. Cyrus's conquest of Babylon and his decree allowing the Jews to return to Judah fulfilled Jeremiah's prophecy of 70 years of captivity.

Second, Jeremiah prophesied God would choose a king of the Medes to destroy Babylon and accomplish His judgment of it (Jer. 51:11). Isaiah had prophesied of Cyrus by name as the one whom God would use to subdue the Babylonian Empire (Isa. 45:1) and support the rebuilding of the temple in Jerusalem (44:28). As king of the Persians and the Medes, Cyrus fulfilled Jeremiah's and Isaiah's prophecies.

After conquering Babylon, Cyrus ruled as king over much of the known biblical world. His army seemed invincible and he seemed able to do whatever he wanted. Yet as powerful as Cyrus was, God possessed all power. While Cyrus believed he acted to accomplish his own desires, he was unknowingly being used of the Lord to accomplish His purposes. Cyrus reigned as a king subject to the King of Kings. God **put it into the mind of King Cyrus to issue a proclamation** that would create a new future for His people.

FOR FURTHER STUDY

Read the article entitled "Cyrus" on pages 377-378 in the *Holman Illustrated Bible Dictionary*. Why do you think the Lord chose to work through Cyrus to accomplish His purpose for His people?

The Persian king used messengers to swiftly deliver proclamations throughout the empire. Typically Persian rulers also issued important decrees in written form that would verify the oral proclamation. The Persians probably wrote the decree in Aramaic, the diplomatic language of their empire. The use of Aramaic would ensure a wide audience could understand the proclamation.

Verse 2: **This is what King Cyrus of Persia says: "The Lord, the God of heaven, has given me all the kingdoms of the earth and has appointed me to build Him a house at Jerusalem in Judah.**

Cyrus's decree might seem to indicate he had become a believer in God but he had not. Cyrus followed a political policy of honoring the customs and religions of his subject peoples. A clay cylinder called the Cyrus Cylinder bears an inscription written after Cyrus's conquest of Babylon. According to the inscription Cyrus portrayed himself as an instrument of the Babylonians' god Marduk and honored the Babylonian gods by restoring their temples. Cyrus willingly credited gods of other nations for his success and sought theses gods' blessings for his empire. By doing so he undoubtedly offended some who believed their gods ruled supreme, but he earned the support of others impressed by his respectful attitude toward their gods.

Cyrus's failure to believe in the Lord did not prevent God from accomplishing His purposes through him. Cyrus adopted a compassionate political policy thinking only of strengthening his empire, but God used Cyrus to accomplish a greater purpose (Prov. 21:1).

The phrase **the God of heaven** referred to the Lord in other Persian decrees (Ezra 7:12,21,23). The Jews also employed the phrase when speaking of God to unbelieving Gentiles (see Ezra 5:12; Jonah 1:9). By using the phrase, Cyrus showed respect for the Lord without expressing sole commitment to Him.

Verse 3: **Whoever is among His people, may his God be with him, and may he go to Jerusalem in Judah and build the house of the Lord, the God of Israel, the God who is in Jerusalem.**

Cyrus granted permission to the Jews to travel to Judah and rebuild their temple and their nation. Cyrus did not forcibly relocate the Jews. Many Jews had made a new, prosperous life for themselves in Babylon. They chose not to go to a place most had never seen and start again. The Lord provided His people with an opportunity but allowed them freedom to decide whether or not to go.

Cyrus's reference to **the God of Israel** and **the God who is in Jerusalem** indicated his belief that God served only as the national Deity of Israel, not of the entire world. Cyrus intended only to pacify a group of his subjects by allowing them to restore their nation and temple. God used Cyrus's limited goal to accomplish His grand purpose.

Verse 4: **Let every survivor, wherever he lives, be assisted by the men of that region with silver, gold, goods, and livestock, along with a freewill offering for the house of God in Jerusalem."**

The **men of that region** referred primarily to the Jews who elected to remain in Babylon although non-Jews might have been included. Cyrus encouraged those who remained behind to provide materials for temple reconstruction and worship. Cyrus's decree probably included provisions for safe conduct to Jerusalem, so Jews who sent valuable gifts could rest assured their fellow Jews and their gifts would arrive safely in Judah.

Verse 5: **So the family leaders of Judah and Benjamin, along with the priests and Levites—everyone God had motivated—prepared to go up and rebuild the LORD's house in Jerusalem.**

Members of three Israelite tribes prepared to leave Babylon. Judah, David's tribe, had comprised the largest part of the Southern Kingdom. Jerusalem's location in Benjamin (see Josh. 18) had linked Judah and Benjamin (2 Chron. 11:1) and the location of the temple in Jerusalem had ensured the presence of many Levites and priests—members of the tribe of Levi—in the city. When the Babylonians deported inhabitants of the Southern Kingdom, representatives from all three tribes had been taken. Cyrus's proclamation accurately reflected the background of the Jewish exiles and indicated the knowledge his officials possessed of their subjects.

The **family leaders** served as heads of extended families much as Abraham had (Gen. 12:5) and would be able to guide the rebuilding and resettling once the Jews arrived in Judah. Those from Judah and Benjamin would reclaim their ancestral lands (Ezra 3:1). The Levites and the priests would supervise the rebuilding of the temple (3:8-9) and reestablish proper worship (3:2-6).

FOR FURTHER STUDY

What individuals in your church have provided steady leadership through the years? How have they seized God-given opportunities?

Only those **God had motivated** needed to leave. God took the initiative, and the people were called to respond. The proclamation provided an opportunity for Jews to reestablish their nation and worship. Those who decided not to return could remain in Babylon and pursue their faith and work.

Verse 6: **All their neighbors supported them with silver articles, gold, goods, livestock, and valuables, in addition to all that was given as a freewill offering.**

When God brought His people out of Egypt in the exodus, the Israelites received gifts from the Egyptians (Ex. 12:35-36). As God brought His people out of Babylon in a second exodus, **their neighbors supported** their return and rebuilding with valuable gifts.

Typically in the Old Testament world when a king conquered a nation, he would take the conquered nation's temple treasures, including the images of their gods, and add them to his treasury. The treasures not only enriched the king but also demonstrated the superiority of his gods over the gods of the conquered nations.

Cyrus returned the things the Babylonians had taken from the Jerusalem temple although, of course, there were no images of God. The items were handled in a serious and careful manner. The Persian treasurer counted out the items to Sheshbazzar [shesh BAZ uhr], the leader of the Jews going to Jerusalem. The figures for the individual categories (Ezra 1:9-10) do not add up to the total number given for all items (1:11). Perhaps the inspired writer listed only the more important items or a representative sample.

Through Cyrus's proclamation God provided His people with a wonderful opportunity to return to their homeland and rebuild the temple. Those who answered God's call to go responded with joy and determination. Those who chose to remain in Babylon responded with gratitude by giving generously to the rebuilding project. Sometimes God calls us to go and serve in a specific ministry and at other times He calls us to stay, pray, and encourage. Like God's people in Babylon, we can respond joyfully, generously, and faithfully.

2. Resettlement in Judah (Ezra 2:1-70)

Life consists of past, present, and future, but too often we live in the present and plan for the future without remembering the past. As the Jews prepared to return to Judah, they needed to remember their connection to the earlier history of Israel and their inheritance of the promises God had made to Abraham. God's plan involved restoring Israel based on His promises of the past.

The same list of families occurs in Nehemiah 7:6-73 with some variations. The purpose of the list may have been to legitimize each family's claim to its land, to distinguish the true descendants of Israel from the Samaritans, or to emphasize the Jews' relationship to God and His plan. The list certainly honors the faith of those who returned.

The list began by emphasizing each family returned to its rightful ancestral land (Ezra 2:1). The names of the leaders followed with some of the leaders having names like those of other biblical figures such as Nehemiah and Mordecai (2:2). The list tied some of the Jews to their ancestors (2:3-20) and others to their ancestral place (2:21-35).

The list of religious personnel followed the list of laypeople. In David's time 24 family groups of priests were recognized (1 Chron. 24:1-19), but only four groups returned to reestablish worship in Jerusalem (Ezra 2:36-39). Even fewer Levites made the journey (2:40-42). Temple servants who performed lesser duties (2:43-54) and other servants (2:55-58) also journeyed to Jerusalem. Others who had lost their ancestral connections or perhaps converted to belief in God while in Babylon accompanied the group (2:59-60). Some from priestly families joined the group but could not serve as priests until their priestly lineage had been established (2:61-63).

The totals given throughout the list do not add up to the final total of 42,360 (2:64). Probably the list reflected only part of the families represented by the Jews who returned to Judah. The mention of slaves and horses indicates some of the Jews possessed wealth but the far larger number of donkeys indicates most were not wealthy (2:65-67). The people gave gifts for the temple based on their ability to give (2:68-69). The Jews settled in their towns but much work remained to be done (2:70).

"Getting there" comprises only part of much that we do. Like the return of the Jews to Jerusalem, our journeys require preparation and courage, but the journey does not complete the job. As God remained with His people, so He remains with us to provide continual courage and guidance.

3. Rebuilding of the Temple Begun (Ezra 3:1-13)

Verse 1: **By the seventh month, the Israelites had settled in their towns, and the people gathered together in Jerusalem.**

The **seventh month**, known as Tishri, equates to the latter part of September and the first part of October in our calendar. More than likely the year was 537 B.C. since the Jews would have required time to prepare and travel back to Judah from Babylon. The seventh month contained several important religious observances. The first day of the month served as New Year and the Festival of Trumpets (Lev. 23:23-25). On the 10th day of the month the Jews celebrated the Day of Atonement (23:26-32) and from the 15th to the 21st day they celebrated the Festival of Booths or Tabernacles followed by a solemn assembly on the 22nd day (23:33-36). Solomon had dedicated his temple during the seventh month (1 Kings 8:2), thus making the seventh month an even more significant time for the returned Jews to reestablish their worship practices in Jerusalem.

The designation **Israelites** originally referred to members of the twelve tribes of Israel. Following the division of the kingdom after Solomon's death, the term *Israel* designated the Northern Kingdom. After the conquest of the Northern Kingdom by the Assyrians in 722 B.C., the term came to be applied to inhabitants of the Southern Kingdom. Although only Jews from the tribes of Judah, Benjamin, and Levi returned to Jerusalem, they comprised the remnant of the original Israel.

The returned Jews had settled in their ancestral towns and begun to rebuild. Then they gathered in Jerusalem to reestablish the worship of God.

Verse 2: **Jeshua son of Jozadak and his brothers the priests along with Zerubbabel son of Shealtiel and his brothers began to build the altar of Israel's God in order to offer burnt offerings on it, as it is written in the law of Moses the man of God.**

The returned Jews began to rebuild the altar under the direction of Jeshua [JESH yoo uh] the high priest, Zerubbabel [zuh RUHB uh buhl] the political leader, and the other priests and officials. Jeshua, son of Jozadak [JAHZ uh dak], was serving as high priest when Babylon destroyed Jerusalem and the Babylonians took him into exile. He must have looked forward to returning to Jerusalem and serving again as priest.

Zerubbabel's grandfather King Jehoiachin had been conquered and taken into exile by the Babylonians in 597 B.C. Zerubbabel, son of Shealtiel [shih AL tih el], made a natural choice for a leader.

God had given the specifications for the tabernacle to Moses shortly after leading His people out of slavery in Egypt. Those instructions detailed the construction of an altar made of wood and covered with bronze (Ex. 27:1-8). Moses later instructed the Israelites to build an altar of uncut stones (Deut. 27:6). The Jews who returned to Jerusalem looked to **the law of Moses** for guidance in building an altar appropriate for worship.

Verse 3: **They set up the altar on its foundation and offered burnt offerings for the morning and evening on it to the LORD even though they feared the surrounding peoples.**

The Jews carefully rebuilt the altar on the exact site of the one built prior to the exile. The altar certainly paled in comparison to the grand altar of Solomon's temple but by building on the exact location of the previous altar the Jews emphasized the continuity of their worship with that of earlier generations and looked toward the Lord's restoring them as He had promised.

After building the altar, the people offered **burnt offerings** in the morning and the evening. With such offerings the entire animal was burned on the altar. This offering symbolized complete dedication to God. God had commanded burnt offerings to be offered each **morning and evening** (Num. 28:3-8). The returning Jews committed themselves to restoring worship not just as a ritual but as an expression of commitment to God.

The Jews worshiped despite their fear of the **surrounding peoples**. During the time the exiles had been in Babylon, foreigners had taken up residence in Judah. The non-Israelites might well have viewed the returning Jews as foreigners who no longer had a right to the land. The returning Jews also faced opposition from those Jews who had remained in Jerusalem and Judah during the exile.

The Festival of Booths was one of Israel's three great annual pilgrimage festivals. The law required every Jewish male to celebrate Passover or the Feast of Unleavened Bread, the Festival of Weeks or Harvest, and the Festival of Booths or Ingathering in Jerusalem (Ex. 23:14-17). The returned Jews endeavored to keep the Festival of Booths precisely as the law stipulated (see Lev. 23:33-36,39-43; Num. 29:12-38). After the Jews had celebrated the Festival of Booths, they continued to offer sacrifices and generously brought freewill offerings to God (Ezra 3:4-5).

Sometimes people begin a project with excitement and enthusiasm but soon lose interest, perhaps because the project becomes more difficult than they initially thought. The task of resettling and rebuilding could easily have made the returned Jews focus on their own lives rather than on worshiping God, but they made corporate worship a priority in their lives. Through private and public worship, God's people maintain a close fellowship with Him that prepares them to live and work for Him confidently in the present and to face the future with hope.

The returning Jews reinstituted the worship of God upon arriving in Jerusalem and then began actively working to purchase supplies and hire the finest craftsmen to rebuild the temple (3:6-7). The returned Jews followed Solomon's example (2 Chron. 2:3-16). Though they lacked Solomon's wealth, they set high standards for the temple's construction and gave generously to the project.

Following Solomon's example (1 Kings 6:1), the Jews also began rebuilding the temple in the second month (Ezra 3:8-9). The second month began the dry season, the perfect time for building. Zerubbabel and Jeshua led in the rebuilding but also appointed Levites to supervise the work. The Levites' great familiarity with ritual purity and the needs of temple worship made them ideal as supervisors.

Verse 10: **When the builders had laid the foundation of the LORD's temple, the priests, dressed in their robes and holding trumpets, and** the Levites descended from Asaph, holding cymbals, took their positions to praise the LORD, as King David of Israel had instructed.

The laying of the foundation in 536 B.C. elicited a response of joy as the people celebrated God and His blessings. The priests and Levites led the people in worship. The descendants of Asaph [AY saf], carrying cymbals, stood in their assigned places ready to lead God's praises. David had appointed Asaph as chief musician to lead in worship. His descendants continued to lead worship through music.

As the Israelites recognized Moses as the one through whom God had established the system of sacrifice, they recognized David as the one through whom God had established music for worship. By following Moses' instructions regarding festivals and sacrifices and David's instructions regarding the use of music for worship, the returned Jews maintained continuity with worship in the temple before the Babylonian exile.

Verse 11: **They sang with praise and thanksgiving to the LORD: "For He is good; His faithful love to Israel endures forever." Then all the people gave a great shout of praise to the LORD because the foundation of the LORD's house had been laid.**

The people joined together singing **with praise and thanksgiving** to God. Songs of praise and thanksgiving celebrate God in general for His nature and actions in creation and history and also praise God for specific acts in the lives of individuals and nations. The refrain **"For He is good; His faithful love to Israel endures forever"** occurs in some of the psalms (see Pss. 106:1; 107:1) and emphasizes God's faithfulness to His covenant.

The people realized the rebuilt altar and temple foundation testified to God's power and faithfulness. Without God's intervention in their history through Cyrus, they would still have been in Babylon. Praising God helps us focus on Him and recognize His hand in our lives. We draw strength from remembering and celebrating God's nature and past actions, especially as we worship surrounded by fellow believers whose testimony enriches and encourages us. Our worship, praise, and confidence in God serve also as a powerful witness to unbelievers. Praise needs to form a vital part of our worship and daily lives. How does praise draw you closer to God?

People of all ages attended the celebration. Some of the older adults remembered Solomon's temple and as they looked at the foundation, they wept. Others among the crowd shouted with enthusiastic joy (Ezra 3:12-13). They had longed for God to restore their nation, city, and temple. The foundation testified to God's faithfulness and a new future for His people.

FOR FURTHER STUDY
What opportunities do you think God is making available for you to serve Him? How can you seize those opportunities?

The Week of December 10

WORKING WITH CONFIDENCE IN GOD

Background Passage: Ezra 4:1–6:22
Lesson Passages: Ezra 4:4-5,24–5:5; 6:8,13-16

INTRODUCTION

The church was located in the middle of the inner city. Ministries to the local community kept it vital and helped the membership grow, but, although the members gave to support their beloved church, they had little to give. The mounting costs for keeping the building repaired and open threatened to close the church.

When the pastor and members believed closing the church constituted their only alternative, the city council recognized the building as a historic landmark. Several civic groups responded by providing funding to preserve the building. With joy the church family celebrated God's provision.

Theresa directed her church's ministry with unwed expectant mothers. The ministry supported women during and after their pregnancy and brought many to salvation in Christ. Often Theresa found herself doing most of the work. As time passed she neared the point of exhaustion.

One Thursday the leader of a women's group in a neighboring church called Theresa and told her the group wanted to help with the ministry— not just with funding but also working with the young women. As Theresa talked with the woman, she offered a silent prayer of thanks.

Sometimes circumstances can overwhelm us as we seek to work for God. We can become so frustrated that we consider abandoning the work and resolving never to involve ourselves in service again. While we may feel abandoned, God does not abandon us. As we rely on Him, He provides us with the courage and perseverance to continue His work. Sometimes He works in unexpected ways to help us accomplish the task He has given us. As did the returned Jewish exiles who rebuilt the temple despite opposition, we also can persevere with God's help.

Ezra 4:1–6:22
1. Facing Opposition (Ezra 4:1-23)
2. Overcoming Hindrances (Ezra 4:24–5:17)
3. Dedicating the Temple (Ezra 6:1-22)

THE BACKGROUND

After the returned exiles laid the foundation for the new temple in Jerusalem, enemies offered to help in the rebuilding process. These enemies were a mixed population, including some Jews who had remained in the land at the time of the exile. Since this mixed population did not possess a pure faith in the Lord (for example, see 2 Kings 17:33), the returned exiles refused their help. In retaliation the enemies bribed Persian officials to frustrate the building effort. Later people from the same area wrote to Persian officials in an attempt to stop the rebuilding of Jerusalem's walls (Ezra 4:1-23).

The enemies' strategy initially proved successful and the building project ceased. After a period of years the prophets Haggai [HAG igh (eye)] and Zechariah [ZEK uh RIGH uh] encouraged the people to resume construction of the temple. Under the guidance of the governor Zerubbabel [zuh RUHB uh buhl] and the priest Jeshua [JESH yoo uh], construction was resumed. When construction resumed, the Persian governor Tattenai [TAT ih nigh] questioned who had given permission for the rebuilding. Tattenai sent a letter to Darius [duh RIGH uhs], king of Persia, that informed him of the rebuilding and of the Jews' statement that Cyrus had given permission for the return of the temple objects and the rebuilding of the temple. While Tattenai waited for Darius's reply, he allowed the rebuilding to continue (4:24 5:17).

A search of the Persian archives uncovered Cyrus's decree. Darius wrote Tattenai confirming the decree and ordering that the tax revenues of Tattenai's area fund the rebuilding and provide sacrificial animals. Tattenai obeyed Darius, and the Jews completed the temple. With great joy the people dedicated the temple and celebrated Passover and the Festival of Unleavened Bread (6:1-22).

THE BIBLE PASSAGE

1. Facing Opposition (Ezra 4:1-23)

The returned Jewish exiles laid the foundation for the new temple with great joy. They probably expected construction to proceed quickly and smoothly, but problems soon surfaced. The Jewish exiles had not returned to an empty land. In the north lived the inhabitants of Samaria, an area formerly occupied by the old Northern Kingdom of Israel. When the Assyrian King Sargon II conquered Israel and destroyed Samaria in 722 B.C., he brought in people from other parts of his empire to help repopulate the area (2 Kings 17:24-33). The descendants of the Israelites who had remained in the land and intermarried with other peoples brought in by the Assyrians became known as the Samaritans. Esarhaddon [EE sahr-HAD uhn], a later Assyrian king, evidently continued the repopulation policy (Ezra 4:2). In the south lived descendants of those few Jews who had not been carried into Babylonian exile.

When the neighbors offered to help with the building, the Jews refused. Their refusal may surprise us. Surely the small community of returned Jews should have welcomed the help and rejoiced to be reunited with their kin. Why would they have been so exclusive?

Two reasons explain the Jews' refusal to accept help. First, the inhabitants of the land worshiped other gods in addition to the Lord. Those Jews whom the Babylonians had not deported also had embraced idolatrous practices. The returned Jews wanted to rebuild a community of faith not make concessions to include anyone who wanted to join no matter their commitment to the Lord. They refused to admit ungodly practices into their community. Today the church too must minister in the world but not by the world's standards.

Second, Cyrus had specifically instructed the Jews in Babylon to return and rebuild their temple (Ezra 4:3). He had not given permission for others to join with them in the rebuilding process.

Verse 4: **Then the people who were already in the land discouraged the people of Judah and made them afraid to build.**

The people who were already in the land reacted quickly and negatively to having their help refused. They **discouraged** those rebuilding the temple. The term *discouraged* translates a Hebrew phrase meaning "relaxing the hands of" or "weakening the hands of." Hands that had shortly before lifted and laid stones sat idle because the Jews were intimidated by the opposition from enemies.

Verse 5: **They also bribed officials ⌊to act⌋ against them to frustrate their plans throughout the reign of King Cyrus of Persia and until the reign of King Darius of Persia.**

The enemies of the returned Jews began a long-term effort to prevent the building of the temple. They **bribed** Persian **officials** to **frustrate** the construction. As a result of the bribes the officials may have raised questions in the Persian court regarding the Jews' intentions, refused to stop the interference of the Jews' enemies, or delayed or discontinued funding for the construction.

The people of the land continued their campaign **throughout the reign of King Cyrus of Persia and until the reign of King Darius of Persia.** The returned Jews laid the temple's foundation in 536 B.C., and Darius became king in 522 B.C. Thus for over a decade intimidation and injustice prevented the temple's completion. The enemies' perseverance in their opposition contrasted with the Jews' lack of perseverance in their rebuilding.

Ezra 4:6-23 refers to further incidents demonstrating the continuing opposition of the people of the land to the Jews in the years after Darius. Ahasuerus, also known as Xerxes I, succeeded his father Darius and ruled from 486 to 465 B.C. During his reign the Jews' enemies continued to write to the Persian king accusing the Jews and halting their attempts to reconstruct their city (Ezra 4:6,16).

Following Ahasuerus's death, his son Artaxerxes became king and ruled from 464 to 424 B.C. Ezra and Nehemiah ministered during Artaxerxes's long reign. Taking advantage of the unrest in the empire at that time, the Samaritans wrote a letter to the king to report that the Jews were rebuilding the walls of Jerusalem and repairing the city's foundations (4:7-12). An unwalled city in the ancient world made itself easy prey for raiders and enemy armies. The Jews certainly would have wanted to restore Jerusalem's wall for protection and prestige, but the Persian government had not given permission for the rebuilding.

Knowing Artaxerxes would not like the Jews engaging in an unapproved project, especially with Jerusalem's proximity to rebellious Egypt, the Samaritans raised two concerns they believed would cause the king to halt the rebuilding. First, the Samaritans suggested that once the Jews rebuilt the city walls and the city, they would withhold their taxes in an act of rebellion and deprive the king of needed income. Second, the Samaritans stated that the Jews had a long history of rebellion and referred the king to the official documents that recorded such rebellions. Hezekiah had rebelled against the Assyrian King Sennacherib about 700 B.C. and Jehoiakim and Zedekiah had revolted against Babylonian kings (2 Kings 24:1,20). The Samaritans stated that if Artaxerxes failed to act, the Jews would rebel again, thus compounding the problems Egypt was already giving the king (Ezra 4:13-16).

After a search of the royal archives seemed to substantiate the Samaritans' concerns, the king instructed the Samaritans to stop the construction in Jerusalem. They quickly responded by forcibly stopping the building (4:17-23).

Why did the inspired writer interrupt the account of the opposition to the rebuilding of the temple to recount later opposition to the rebuilding of Jerusalem's wall? Probably the writer wanted to demonstrate both the constancy of the opposition throughout many years and over the long reigns of several Persian kings and the true character of the people of the land. The term *enemy* accurately identified the people of Samaria. Their hatred of the Jews ran so deep that generations continued their fanatical opposition to the restoration of Judah.

Today Christians face opposition from many sources. Opposition in some nations can take the form of physical and economic persecution. In nations that enjoy religious freedom, opposition often proves more subtle. Churches that seek to follow God by taking unpopular stands and engaging in ministry may suffer vandalism, discrimination against members, and unfounded rumors. Some opposition may be internal as disagreements lead to anger, hatred, and even church splits.

We should not be surprised when we face opposition. Jesus told His disciples that if people persecuted Him, they would also persecute them (John 15:20). Christians inevitably face opposition because the world resists the teachings of Jesus. We need to anticipate frustrations in following Christ and prepare to face opposition with courage and compassion.

FOR FURTHER STUDY

Read the article entitled "Samaria, Samaritans" on pages 1435-1437 in the *Holman Illustrated Bible Dictionary*. What would have made the Jews of Ezra's time and the Jews of Jesus' time reluctant to work with the Samaritans?

2. Overcoming Hindrances (Ezra 4:24–5:17)

Chapter 4. Verse 24: **Now the construction of God's house in Jerusalem had stopped and remained at a standstill until the second year of the reign of King Darius of Persia.**

After describing the later opposition to the rebuilding of the city wall, the inspired writer returned to the situation of the Jews under the new King Darius (see 4:5). When Cyrus died, Cambyses II [kam BIGH seez] succeeded him and ruled from 530 to 522 B.C. Darius had served as an officer under Cambyses and campaigned with him in Egypt. Following Cambyses's untimely death, Darius established himself as king by claiming kinship to Cyrus. Darius spent the first few years of his long reign (522-486 B.C.) crushing rebellions and then led the Persian Empire to its greatest power and glory.

Cyrus had provided permission and funding to rebuild the temple and the Jews had laid the foundation, but opposition had brought construction to a halt. The **second year of the reign of King Darius of Persia** would have been 520 B.C. so for about 16 years the Jews had failed to make progress on the temple. They had focused on their own livelihood and comfort and given up on rebuilding their place of worship (Hag. 1:4).

Chapter 5. Verse 1: **But when the prophets Haggai and Zechariah son of Iddo prophesied to the Jews who were in Judah and Jerusalem, in the name of the God of Israel who was over them,**

God used two prophets to encourage the Jews to renew the building of the temple. Haggai's written prophecies date from August to December

520. Haggai scolded the Jews for working on their own houses but neglecting the temple (Hag. 1:2-4). Their neglect of the temple constituted a neglect of God. Haggai challenged the people to renew their efforts on the temple and experience God's blessing (1:5-11). He also assured the people of God's presence with them despite the opposition they faced (1:13).

Zechariah, **son of Iddo** [ID oh], prophesied during the period 520-518 B.C. Here the word *son* means "descendant" because Zechariah identified Iddo as his grandfather (Zech. 1:1,7). Nehemiah listed Iddo as one of the priests among those who returned from exile (Neh. 12:4,16). Like Haggai, Zechariah called his people back to God by reminding them of what God had done to earlier disobedient generations (Zech. 1:2-6). He also assured the Jews of God's presence and of the ultimate success of their temple rebuilding (4:9-10).

The word **them** in the phrase **the God of Israel who was over them** could apply either to the prophets or to the people but probably applies to both. God had called and directed the prophets to proclaim His message to the people. God also reigned over the people. For the moment Darius ruled them, but God ruled them eternally.

Verse 2: Zerubbabel son of Shealtiel and Jeshua son of Jozadak began to rebuild God's house in Jerusalem. The prophets of God were with them, helping them.

Both the Jews and their leaders responded to Haggai's and Zechariah's words. Zerubbabel was part of the first group of Jews to return to Judah from Babylon. As the son of Shealtiel [shih AL tih el] and the grandson of Jehoiachin—the king of Judah whom the Babylonians had taken into exile and who was still viewed as the legitimate king—Zerubbabel would naturally have risen to leadership in the community. By the second year of Darius, Zerubbabel was serving as governor in Judah (Hag. 1:1). Jeshua or Joshua, son of Jozadak [JAHZ uh dak], served as high priest in Jerusalem (1:1; 2:2). Both had helped lay the temple's foundation (Ezra 3:8) and led in the rebuilding.

The **prophets of God** certainly referred to Haggai and Zechariah but may have included other unnamed prophets. The prophets encouraged the Jews to renew the construction and the governor and high priest coordinated the rebuilding. God used the abilities of many people to accomplish His purpose.

Verse 3: At that time Tattenai the governor of the region west of the Euphrates River, Shethar-bozenai, and their colleagues came to the Jews

and asked, "Who gave you the order to rebuild this temple and finish this structure?"

No sooner had the Jews renewed the rebuilding of the temple than Persian officials came to Jerusalem to investigate. Tattenai served as **governor of the region west of the Euphrates** [yoo FRAY teez] **River**. The term *governor* is used rather broadly in this context. As governor of Judah, Zerubbabel exercised authority over a small area. Tattenai's authority included all of biblical Palestine. Even Tattenai did not answer directly to Darius but most likely to a satrap, a higher official. Shethar-bozenai [SHEE thahr-BAHZ ih nigh] probably served as Tattenai's secretary. The presence of Tattenai accompanied by his secretary and other officials certainly would have made the Jews nervous.

Seeing the construction, Tattenai asked who had given permission for the rebuilding. Bible scholars have suggested several reasons for Tattenai's visit and questions. Some believe the Samaritans had again accused the Jews with the result that Tattenai decided to investigate. Others think the Jews might have tried to crown Zerubbabel, a descendant of David, as their king and brought Tattenai's attention upon themselves. However, the Old Testament does not mention an attempt to crown Zerubbabel. Still other scholars suggest Tattenai visited Jerusalem as part of a routine inspection tour. When he saw the construction, he naturally asked whether the Jews had received official permission for the project.

Verse 4: They also asked them, "What are the names of the workers who are constructing this building?"

As a follow-up question, Tattenai asked for the names of the individuals working on the project. He wanted to provide as much information as possible to Darius.

Verse 5: But God was watching over the Jewish elders. These men wouldn't stop them until a report was sent to Darius, so that they could receive written instructions about this ⌊matter⌋.

Tattenai filed a report with Darius and awaited the king's instructions. The process of sending the report, having officials search the royal records, and receiving Darius's reply would take four to five months. Tattenai gave the Jews permission to continue their construction during the interim.

Tattenai's allowing rebuilding to continue resulted from God's care of His people. The phrase **God was watching over** translates the Hebrew expression "the eye of their God was on." The people of the Persian Empire often referred to inspectors and governors like Tattenai as the king's eyes and ears. They traveled through the empire inspecting and reporting what they found to the king. In contrast to Darius who needed officials to serve as his eyes and ears, God needed no one to serve as His eyes and ears. He saw and knew everything and was acting so His people could complete their work for Him. As the Jews awaited Darius's answer, they could continue their work assured of God's sustaining presence.

To achieve the rebuilding of the temple, God used the challenging preaching of the prophets, the leadership of the governor and high priest, the dedicated work of the Jewish community, and the decisions of unbelievers. God works in various ways today. Through personal and group Bible study, Christians experience God's call to specific service. Testimonies and sermons provide further encouragement and direction. God raises up leaders to plan, coordinate, and implement ministries and provides support from various, and sometimes surprising, groups. When God calls, we can follow with the confidence He is working with us and supplying our needs.

Tattenai sent a letter to Darius containing a balanced report of the facts he had gleaned from the Jews. He noted the two questions he had asked (Ezra 5:6-10). Tattenai then presented the Jews' response regarding their permission to build the temple. The Jews emphasized their belief in and loyalty to God and indicated they were rebuilding the temple a previous great king had built but that had been destroyed. The Jews did not blame the destruction on Babylonian power and cruelty. They recognized their sin as the cause of Jerusalem's destruction and their deportation. The Jews then reported Cyrus's decree allowing them to return to Judah with the temple vessels the Babylonians had taken and rebuild the temple. The reference to Sheshbazzar provided a specific name that might help Darius's officials locate Cyrus's decree concerning the Jews. Finally the Jews acknowledged the slow progress of the rebuilding. Tattenai asked Darius to search the royal archives to determine the accuracy of the Jews' claim. Darius could then send instructions to Tattenai (Ezra 5:11-17).

Sometimes we might be able to overcome certain obstacles to accomplishing personal or ministry goals. We might be able to find the training we need, raise support, or rearrange our schedules. Some hindrances only God can overcome. In times of despair only God can provide us with the strength and courage we need. In times of frustration only God can give us the perseverance to carry on. God can and does work miracles to accomplish His purposes.

FOR FURTHER STUDY
How do you think Christians should respond when challenged regarding their activities?

3. Dedicating the Temple (Ezra 6:1-22)

The rebellions in parts of Darius's empire that had occupied his first years as king would have encouraged him to take seriously Tattenai's report regarding possibly unapproved construction. Darius's officials eventually found a copy of Cyrus's decree in the archives in Ecbatana [ehk BAT uh nuh], the Persian summer palace (Ezra 6:1-2).

Although the decree in Ezra 6:3-5 differs from the one recorded in Ezra 1:2-4, both agree in the essentials and may be summaries of a more detailed official document. The decree given here provides more specific information regarding the location and construction of the temple. The decree also noted the method for financing the construction. Darius ordered Tattenai and his officials not to interfere in the temple rebuilding (6:6-7).

Verse 8: I hereby issue a decree concerning what you must do, so that the elders of the Jews can rebuild this house of God: The cost is to be paid in full to these men out of the royal revenues from the taxes of the region west of the Euphrates River, so that the ⌊work⌋ will not stop.

Darius not only upheld Cyrus's decree but issued a decree himself providing permission and funding for the construction and animals for sacrifices. The king instructed Tattenai to fund the project and temple worship from **the royal revenues from the taxes of the region west of the Euphrates River,** the area Tattenai administered. Darius's policy kept his Jewish subjects satisfied and gave them a sense of freedom. In return Darius asked the Jews to pray for him and his sons (6:9-10).

Ancient covenants often included curses on those who dared to break the agreement. Impalement served as a particularly horrible method of execution. One end of a wooden beam, in this case from the individual's house, would be sharpened. The other end would be placed in the ground. The victim was then placed on the sharpened end so the point went under the rib cage and into the lungs and esophagus. Death was agonizing. An additional curse applied to anyone, royal or not, who would attempt to halt construction of the temple (6:11-12).

Verse 13: Then Tattenai governor of the region west of the Euphrates River, Shethar-bozenai, and their colleagues diligently carried out what King Darius had decreed.

Tattenai quickly moved to obey Darius. If Tattenai had hoped to stop the construction, perhaps at the Samaritans' request, he knew he could not.

Verse 14: So the Jewish elders continued successfully with the building under the prophesying of Haggai the prophet and Zechariah son of Iddo. They finished the building according to the command of the God of Israel and the decrees of Cyrus, Darius, and King Artaxerxes of Persia.

This verse reveals that the Lord worked through various individuals to accomplish His purposes. In the Persian Empire, the king's decree held sway. Yet as powerful as Darius was, One existed who had all power. In the list of the kings who supported the restoration of Jerusalem and Judah, God occupied first place. He worked through the decisions of kings, as subordinate to Him as a citizen of Judah would have been to Darius, to accomplish His purpose. What appeared to be the gracious decree of Darius was in reality the gracious act of God.

Verse 15: This house was completed on the third day of the month of Adar in the sixth year of the reign of King Darius.

The Jews completed the temple in 516 B.C., approximately 70 years after the Babylonians had destroyed it. Jeremiah's prophecy of the 70-year exile proved remarkably accurate (Jer. 29:10). Solomon's temple had stood for almost four hundred years. The new temple, with Herod's later renovations, would stand for well over five hundred, finally experiencing destruction at the hands of the Roman general Titus. Through prophets, governors, priests, kings, and faithful believers, God worked a miracle that would serve as a long-lasting testament to His love and power.

Verse 16: Then the Israelites, including the priests, the Levites, and the rest of the exiles, celebrated the dedication of this house of God with joy.

The Jews marked the temple's completion with a joyous celebration and **dedication**. The Hebrew word translated *dedication* is "Hanukkah," the name of the Jewish festival celebrated in December that commemorates the rededication of the temple in 165 B.C. after Judas Maccabeus cleansed it from the pollution of pagan worship. Although the offerings accompanying the dedication of the temple totaled far fewer than those Solomon offered at his temple's dedication (see 1 Kings 8:63), they represented a significant sacrifice from the small Jewish community. Having given their best in construction, the people gave their best in offerings. The Jews offered a sin offering for each tribe, thereby underscoring their identification as the true Israel. The people then organized the religious officials according to Moses' instructions (Ezra 6:17-18).

Soon after the dedication, the people gathered to joyfully celebrate Passover and the Feast of Unleavened Bread. As they celebrated, their current situation as exiles returning home and worshiping in the temple must have reminded them of God's miraculous deliverance of His people from Egyptian slavery. That Pharaoh would have allowed the Israelites to leave Egypt seemed impossible, but God had accomplished His purpose. That the exiles would return to Jerusalem, rebuild the temple, and worship there again must also have seemed impossible, but again God had accomplished His will. When we face opposition today, we can be confident of God's presence and work to accomplish His will. We can confidently persevere in our ministry with the assurance that God will fulfill His purposes through us.

FOR FURTHER STUDY

As you think about opposition facing you or your church, list two resources you have for confidently persevering in God's service.

The Week of December 17

FOLLOWING GODLY SPIRITUAL LEADERS

Background Passage: Ezra 7:1–10:44
Lesson Passages: Ezra 7:8-10; 9:1-2,4; 10:1-5

INTRODUCTION

Let's begin with a quiz! Of the four individuals listed below, which ones would you identify as godly leaders?

Pastor A—When church leaders began to talk about a new building, Pastor A expressed excitement although the church had sufficient space. The more he prayed about the building, the more he believed the money could better be spent elsewhere. He led the church to express thanks for their current facilities and collect an offering to build a mission church.

Youth Minister B—Youth Minister B planned great activities and led popular Bible studies but typically spent time with only a few youth, while ignoring the others. When parents expressed concern, he denied everything, yelled at them, and told them not to challenge his authority.

Deacon C—Deacon C led his church in forming ministry teams so members could exercise their spiritual gifts. Several months later the church discovered he had committed adultery with a choir member's wife.

Sunday School Teacher D—Sunday School Teacher D's class maintained a flower fund so they could send flowers to those who were ill or had experienced loss. Teacher D personally delivered the flowers, always taking another member of the class with her and offering prayer for the individual. She continued to visit and help meet further needs.

As much as we might like to think otherwise, not all Christian leaders are godly leaders. Their failings can display themselves in financial mismanagement, sexual infidelity, anger, apathy, or other ungodly behaviors.

Godly spiritual leaders do more than know the Bible's teaching. They constantly examine their lives for sin, live by God's truth, and prayerfully guide others. Ezra provides a model of a godly spiritual leader.

Ezra 7:1–10:44
1. Returning to Jerusalem (Ezra 7:1–8:36)
2. Confessing Sin (Ezra 9:1-15)
3. Turning from Sin (Ezra 10:1-44)

THE BACKGROUND

Ezra's arrival in Jerusalem occurred 58 years after the completion and dedication of the temple in 516 B.C. King Artaxerxes of Persia sent Ezra, a priestly descendant of Aaron, to teach Moses' law to those in Judah. Ezra made an ideal choice for the task because he intensely studied God's law and sought to apply it in his life. The king provided funding for Ezra's journey and for temple needs, encouraged Jews in Babylon to give generously, and eliminated taxes for Jewish religious leaders. Other Jews decided to accompany Ezra. For three days they camped by the Ahava River, while Ezra successfully recruited Levites to accompany the group. Before leaving, Ezra prayed for a safe journey and carefully recorded all the valuables that had been given for use in the Jerusalem temple. After traveling several months, Ezra and his fellow Jews arrived in Jerusalem, rested, and delivered the treasures to the temple (Ezra 7:1–8:36).

Later the leaders brought a serious problem to Ezra's attention. Some of the people, including some religious leaders, had married non-Jews, thereby opening themselves and their children to the sin of idolatry. Ezra reacted with grief and silence followed by a prayer of confession (9:1-15).

While Ezra prayed and confessed the people's sins, many gathered and wept. Shecaniah [SHEK uh NIGH uh], a leader, believed God would forgive the people if they confessed and repented of their sins. He suggested sending the foreign wives and their children away thus removing the sin and purifying the community. The leaders supported Shecaniah's solution, and Ezra had the people swear an oath to abide by the decision. The leaders called all the men of Judah to gather in Jerusalem. As the men met, they decided to conduct a calm, thorough investigation. A three-month investigation yielded a list of men who had sinned, and they responded by sending away their non-Jewish wives and children (10:1-44).

FOR FURTHER STUDY

Read the article entitled "Ezra" on page 542 of the *Holman Illustrated Bible Dictionary*. Why was and is Ezra so important?

THE BIBLE PASSAGE

1. Returning to Jerusalem (Ezra 7:1–8:36)

Artaxerxes I of Persia ruled from 464 to 424 B.C. so Ezra arrived in Jerusalem long after the completion and dedication of the temple under Darius (6:16-22). The list of Ezra's ancestors highlighted only some of his forefathers on the way to tracing his lineage back to Aaron, Moses' brother and the first high priest. Interestingly Azariah, mentioned twice in the list, shared the same root name as Ezra. "Ezra" constituted a shortened form of the name Azariah meaning "the Lord has helped."

Despite Jewish migration to Jerusalem, a strong Jewish community remained in Babylon. The Jews in Babylon worshiped God and studied God's law. Obviously the community possessed, studied, and treasured the Torah (Genesis through Deuteronomy) and probably possessed and studied some of the Prophets and other Old Testament Writings.

The term *scribe* that described Ezra originally referred to a secretary who functioned in the royal court (2 Sam. 20:25; 2 Kings 22:3), but the designation *scribe* came to refer to an individual who invested his life in Scripture through studying, interpreting, and copying. In the person of Ezra, the two meanings are combined. Artaxerxes gave him a high office involving the enforcement of Jewish law in Judah. At the same time, Ezra's expertise in God's law came from intensive study. With Ezra the emphasis on a scribe as an expert in and teacher of God's law became far more important than the scribe having status in the royal court. The scribes of Jesus' time continued the tradition of scholarship and teaching begun by Ezra.

As God had worked through Cyrus to allow Jews to return to Jerusalem and through Cyrus and Darius to rebuild the temple, God also worked through Artaxerxes to provide the Jews of Judah with a spiritual leader. The Lord's hand rested on Ezra. As a result his work prospered, and God's purposes were fulfilled.

Verse 8: Ezra came to Jerusalem in the fifth month, during the seventh year of the king.

Artaxerxes I ruled Persia for approximately 40 years. Although ruthless in securing his empire and initially opposed to Nehemiah's rebuilding of Jerusalem's walls (Ezra 4:18-22), he supported the work of Ezra and Nehemiah in Judah. Under the auspices of Artaxerxes I, Ezra arrived in Jerusalem in 458 B.C.

Verse 9: He began the journey from Babylon on the first day of the first month and arrived in Jerusalem on the first day of the fifth month. The gracious hand of his God was on him,

Ezra began his journey **on the first day of the first month** and reached Jerusalem **on the first day of the fifth month**. The dates marked significant anniversaries for the Jews. Centuries earlier God had led Israel out of Egypt in the *first month* (Ex. 12:2). More than a century before Ezra's journey the Babylonian army had destroyed the Jerusalem temple in the *fifth month* (2 Kings 25:8-9). The journey of Ezra's group served as a new exodus for Ezra and his group as God continued to restore His people. Ezra's group probably traveled northwest following the Euphrates River and then down through Syria and into Jerusalem. The presence of bandits, rugged terrain, and heat made the journey difficult. As God had protected the people of Israel in their journey out of Egypt and into Canaan, so His **gracious hand** protected Ezra's group as they traveled to Jerusalem.

Verse 10: **because Ezra had determined in his heart to study the law of the LORD, obey ⌊it⌋, and teach ⌊its⌋ statutes and ordinances in Israel.**

Artaxerxes sent Ezra to Jerusalem to organize the community around God's law (Ezra 7:25-26). Artaxerxes could have chosen no better person. Ezra had **determined in his heart to study the law of the LORD**. Since the Jews believed decision-making occurred in the heart, the verse emphasizes that Ezra had chosen to focus his entire life on God's law.

Ezra's commitment to God evidenced itself in three ways. First, he studied God's law. The word **study** translates a Hebrew word also meaning "seek." Seeking implies more than just being familiar with or even memorizing. Ezra diligently sought to understand the spirit of God's law and how to apply the law in daily life.

Second, Ezra obeyed God's law. Ezra realized God expected His people to live according to His law and to apply His guidance in daily life. Faith does not consist of an intellectual pursuit but of a transformed life lived daily for God.

Third, Ezra taught God's law. God's people need teachers to remind them of the importance of following God's standards and to help them learn how to apply God's law in daily life. **Statutes** refer to rules of conduct and **ordinances** refer to duties that lead to righteous and just living. Together statutes and ordinances encompass all of God's law.

Ezra serves as a wonderful example of a godly leader. He invested his life in studying God's Word, living by God's Word, and teaching God's Word to others. Ezra practiced what he preached. His life and words testified to his commitment to God and gave his teaching a power and honesty that drew people to follow God.

Artaxerxes gave Ezra a letter to serve as his credentials from the king. Persian rulers liked to refer to themselves by the title "king of kings" (7:12) although the title only legitimately refers to Christ (Rev. 17:14). The letter contained five sections. The first section (Ezra 7:13-14) granted permission for Ezra and his fellow Jews to go to Jerusalem and empowered Ezra to teach and enforce God's law in Judah. Persian rulers typically encouraged their subjects to follow their own laws as long as the laws did not conflict with Persian law.

The next three sections dealt with financial matters. The second section (7:15-20) provided gifts for the temple and financing to purchase sacrifices and provide for temple upkeep. In the third section Artaxerxes commanded the treasurers of the districts west of the Euphrates River to provide for Ezra (7:21-23). The king's generous gifts indicated the Persians' desire to support the religions of their subjects and to meet the needs of

Ezra's group along the journey. The fourth section (7:24) mandated the typical Persian policy of exempting religious personnel from taxation.

The final section (7:25-26) empowered Ezra to establish a system of judges who would help apply God's law to all Jews living in the area west of the Euphrates River. The king promised the full power of Persian law and enforcement to support the application of God's law. Receiving the letter, Ezra joyously gave thanks to God (7:27-28).

The list of those who joined Ezra included representatives from two priestly families (8:2a), David's line (8:2b), and 12 additional families (8:3-14). The group camped near the Ahava River or canal to make final preparations for the trip. Ezra organized the group and discovered a complete absence of Levites. The Levites performed rather menial tasks in the temple,' and many probably had more satisfying work and status in Babylon. Ezra managed to recruit 38 Levites and a large group of temple servants to assist the Levites (8:15-20).

After gathering the people, Ezra proclaimed a fast and time of prayer for a safe journey. Leaving the known of Babylon for the unknown of Jerusalem took courage and faith. Ezra prayed and God answered his prayer (8:21-23).

Like all good leaders Ezra chose people of integrity and delegated responsibilities to them. Ezra and the leaders weighed the valuables, noted their number and worth, and guarded the treasure carefully (8:24-30). After arriving and resting from the long, difficult journey, Ezra weighed out the valuables to Meremoth the priest. Nothing had been lost. Following a time of worship, Ezra showed his credentials to the satraps and governors and began his service to God and king (8:31-36).

FOR FURTHER STUDY

List three godly leaders you have known. What characteristics made them godly leaders?

2. Confessing Sin (Ezra 9:1-15)

Verse 1: **After these things had been done, the leaders approached me and said: "The people of Israel, the priests, and the Levites have not separated themselves from the surrounding peoples whose detestable practices are like those of the Canaanites, Hittites, Perizzites, Jebusites, Ammonites, Moabites, Egyptians, and Amorites.**

Ezra and his group arrived in Jerusalem on the first day of the fifth month. The events in Ezra 9–10 occurred in the ninth month (10:9) so four months passed before the leaders brought the problem to Ezra's attention. Perhaps Ezra had been involved in teaching, while hoping his explanation of God's law would convict the community, and they would recognize and confess their sins.

A group of Jewish leaders informed Ezra that some Jews had **not separated themselves from the surrounding peoples**. The leaders provided a sample list of inhabitants of biblical Palestine similar to lists found elsewhere in the Old Testament (see Gen. 15:19-21; Ex. 3:8). The old lists typically did not mention the Ammonites, Moabites, and Egyptians, so their inclusion by the leaders reflected the present situation. The other groups no longer existed as such, but their names are used here in a representative sense to refer to all surrounding pagan peoples. The list applied God's law to the present day.

After God brought His people out of Egypt, He instructed them not to make a treaty with the nations in Canaan. He also told His people to destroy the pagan worship sites so the Israelites would not be tempted by their **detestable practices** (Ex. 34:12-14). Unfortunately God's people had not obeyed Him, they had become entangled in idolatry, and they had suffered the consequences. The leaders reported that some of the Jews in Judah refused to obey God and learn from the past. The participation of religious leaders, priests and Levites, in the practice made matters worse.

Verse 2: **Indeed, they have taken some of their daughters as wives for themselves and their sons, so that the holy people has become mixed with the surrounding peoples. The leaders and officials have taken the lead in this unfaithfulness!"**

The problem went further than fellowship with other groups or participation in their idolatrous rituals. Jewish men had married foreign women who practiced idolatry. The Old Testament did not completely forbid Israelites to marry foreigners. Joseph married an Egyptian (Gen. 41:45). Boaz married Ruth, a Moabitess, who became a faithful believer in God and an ancestress of David (Ruth 4:13-17). Yet even the patriarchs expressed a desire that their sons not marry Canaanite women (Gen. 24:2-4; 28:1-9).

God prohibited intermarriage with the Canaanites because their idolatrous practices would lead the Israelites away from God (Ex. 34:15-16). Solomon's marriages to foreign women brought their idolatry into Jerusalem and led Solomon astray (1 Kings 11:1-8). Ahab's foreign wife Jezebel led Ahab and Israel astray (1 Kings 16:31-33).

God did not base His prohibition on racial or ethnic prejudice. God's prohibition focused purely on religious purity. **Unfaithfulness** revealed the true problem. The term *unfaithfulness* was used to refer to a broken covenant with God (Lev. 26:40). God had called His people to be holy or to be separated to Him (Ex. 19:6). His people stood in danger of repeating the past sins that had led their nation into defeat and exile.

As we think about the issue of marriages to people of different faiths, we need to remember God does not want us to retreat from the world. We need to be in the world bearing testimony for Christ, but we need to be distinctly different, committed to and separated for God's use, holy to Him. To be that kind of people, we need the support of fellow believers in our homes and in our churches.

FOR FURTHER STUDY

God has called believers to be holy. What actions can compromise our Christian witness and hinder our fellowship with God? How can we avoid such actions?

Ezra responded to the leaders' report by tearing his tunic and robe and pulling hair out of his head and beard (Ezra 9:3). His actions demonstrated his great concern and grief. Artaxerxes had sent him to enforce God's law among the Jews and after only four months he had been alerted to a significant infraction of God's law.

Verse 4: Everyone who trembled at the words of the God of Israel gathered around me, because of the unfaithfulness of the exiles, while I sat devastated until the evening offering.

Ezra's actions drew a crowd, not of curious onlookers but of **everyone who trembled at the words of the God of Israel**. The group that surrounded Ezra consisted of people who sought to understand God's law and obey Him. Having recognized the sin, they mourned with Ezra and waited for further instruction from him. Ezra remained in deep mourning until the time of the **evening offering**, about 3:00 p.m. The *evening offering* served as a time of prayer (Acts 3:1) and provided a perfect time for Ezra to intercede for his people.

Ezra rose up from his mourning and knelt with his hands stretched out to God. His posture indicated his humility before God and his need for God's help. Ezra offered a beautiful prayer. His prayer began with a confession of sin (Ezra 9:6-7a). Although he had not married a foreign wife, he identified with his people, including himself as one of the sinners. Ezra then referred to the judgment Israel and Judah had suffered for their idolatrous ways (9:7b). Both nations had experienced defeat. Judah had experienced an exile from which Jews were still returning to their ancestral land.

Defeat, however, had not been God's last word. Ezra noted God had preserved a remnant of His people, allowed the exiles to return home, and used the Persians to help rebuild the temple and the city (9:8-9). Yet the remnant had become impure, and history was in danger of repeating itself. Ezra again confessed his people's sins and noted the seriousness of their disobedience as well as its possible consequences (9:10-14). Ezra concluded by recognizing only God's righteousness evidenced in His forgiveness had enabled a remnant to survive (9:15; see 1 John 1:9).

The Jewish leaders who had married foreign wives classified themselves as ungodly leaders by their sinful behavior. Some may not have joined the group that surrounded Ezra and mourned with him because they saw nothing wrong in their actions. By contrast, Ezra grieved for his people, identified with them, confessed their sins, and reminded them of God's law, the nation's history, and God's forgiveness. Godly leaders consistently study God's Word, apply His Word to their lives, identify with their followers as fellow sinners, confess sin, pray for forgiveness, and seek to mature in faith.

3. Turning from Sin (Ezra 10:1-44)

Verse 1: While Ezra prayed and confessed, weeping and falling face-down before the house of God, an extremely large assembly of Israelite men, women, and children gathered around him. The people also wept bitterly.

Ezra had offered a powerful prayer of confession (Ezra 9:6-15). As he prayed, he wept and prostrated himself before the temple. No wonder a crowd gathered. Ezra was a respected figure partially because of the authority Artaxerxes had given him but primarily because of his commitment to God and teaching His law. News of the great teacher's grief would have spread quickly throughout Jerusalem and drawn a large group of people.

The large crowd that gathered around Ezra may have included some of the wives and children of the mixed-faith marriages. Recognizing their sin, the crowd **wept bitterly** with Ezra. The people recognized the problem constituted a crisis for the whole community and not just for isolated individuals. As a community problem, the community's inhabitants needed to deal with it as they looked to Ezra for leadership.

Verse 2: Then Shecaniah son of Jehiel, an Elamite, responded to Ezra: "We have been unfaithful to our God by marrying foreign women from the surrounding peoples, but there is still hope for Israel in spite of this.

From the crowd stepped a leader, Shecaniah [SHEK uh NIGH uh], an Elamite and the son of Jehiel, to offer hope and a solution. Later investigation discovered six descendants of Elam, including a man named Jehiel [jih HIGH el], who had married foreign wives (10:26). Although we cannot know for sure, Shecaniah's own father might have been one of the culprits and Shecaniah might have been an adult child of his father's mixed-faith marriage. Shecaniah had followed a different path, seeking to follow God's law, but he knew others in his own clan had disobeyed God.

Shecaniah presented a plan of action. Like Ezra, he identified with his sinful people and confessed their sin. Then remembering God's grace in preserving a remnant and bringing His people home to Judah, he suggested the Jews might still have hope in spite of their disobedience. The people's hope rested in God's grace.

Verse 3: Let us therefore make a covenant before our God to send away all the ⌊foreign⌋ wives and their children, according to the counsel of my lord and of those who tremble at the commandment of our God. Let it be done according to the law.

Shecaniah suggested a drastic solution. The community needed to identify and then send away **all the foreign wives and their children**. The action needed to be accomplished **according to the law**. God had instructed His people not to marry the inhabitants of the land because the Israelites would fall prey to their idolatry (Deut. 7:3-4). The current mixed-faith marriages clearly disobeyed God's command. God's law also provided permission to divorce a wife, if the husband discovered "something improper about her" (Deut. 24:1). Idolatry would certainly qualify as "something improper," and thus the Jews believed divorce comprised the best course of action in this situation.

Shecaniah's suggestion seems harsh. The disruption of families through divorce hardly seems to us like a reasonable or best solution. Knowing the destructive power of divorce, we struggle to salvage marriages through counseling, prayer, and encouragement.

Ezra and the Jews faced a desperate situation. Their history had demonstrated the destructiveness of idolatry. In order not to repeat history and incur God's further wrath and judgment, the wives had to go. The children went with their mothers.

Shecaniah's plan spoke to the need of a particular historical situation. His suggestion did not lay down a law for all time that gives us license to divorce an unbelieving spouse. While believers are commanded not to be unequally yoked with unbelievers (2 Cor. 6:14), there are situations in which one partner becomes a believer while the other does not. In those situations, believing spouses need to allow their love and faithfulness to their marriage partners to witness to God's love and offer of abundant life.

On the other hand, those who have experienced the tragedy of divorce do not need to be treated as though they have committed the unpardonable sin. They need to be assured of God's love and the church's care and support. In the Old Testament world, a woman's father or brother typically served as the woman's guardian to ensure that the husband kept the marriage contract. The Jews might have arranged for the guardians of the wives to care for the wives and the children. In today's world, the church needs to care for single parents and their children by offering support, encouragement, and care.

Verse 4: Get up, for this matter is your responsibility, and we support you. Be strong and take action!"

Knowing Ezra possessed the authority to solve the problem (Ezra 7:26), Shecaniah encouraged him to act. Shecaniah pledged the support of the leaders as Ezra implemented the plan.

Verse 5: **Then Ezra got up and made the leading priests, Levites, and all Israel take an oath to do what had been said; so they took the oath.**

Ezra made **the leading priests, Levites, and all Israel take an oath** to commit to the plan. Ezra and the people knew they could not deal with the sin that day. They needed to investigate so as not to accuse someone unjustly. Yet the people needed to commit themselves before the conviction of the moment faded. Realizing their sin and knowing Shecaniah's plan provided the best means to deal with their disobedience, the people **took the oath**.

When we encounter godly leaders, we need to follow them knowing they help us follow God. When godly leaders identify our sins, we need to confess and repent. When they interpret God's Word to us, we need to apply God's Word to our lives and obey. As they lead us, we need to encourage and support them with our prayers, cooperation, and finances. Godly leaders help us become more of what God has called us to be. We need to give thanks for them and support them.

FOR FURTHER STUDY

What difficult decision have the leaders of your church had to make? How did they involve the congregation in making and abiding by the decision?

The leaders called all the exiles to assemble in Jerusalem. Those who chose not to come would forfeit the loss of their possessions and experience exclusion from the community. The severity of the sin necessitated the presence of all Jews to confess, repent, investigate, and act (Ezra 10:6-8).

As the people assembled in the temple area, they trembled as a result of Judah's great sin and a heavy rain. They confessed their sin but recognized they could not act to solve the horrible problem in a day or two. Enacting Shecaniah's plan necessitated a calm case-by-case assessment. The people suggested appointing the leaders to investigate each individual accused of marrying a foreign wife. With majority approval, the leaders began their work (10:9-17). The investigation required three months and the community sent the wives and children of the guilty men away (10:18-44).

Leaders and followers sometimes have to make difficult decisions. Like Ezra and the Jewish leaders, we need to exercise caution and act with integrity. We must accomplish God's purpose with redemptive compassion.

FOR FURTHER STUDY

List the characteristics you will look for in godly leaders and then describe ways you will support them.

The Week of December 24

HONORING THE SAVIOR'S BIRTH

Background Passage: Matthew 1:18–2:12
Lesson Passages: Matthew 1:18–2:5a,9-11

INTRODUCTION

On Friday, July 16, 2004, I sat with a group of American believers in the church in Penglai, China where the great Southern Baptist missionary Charlotte "Lottie" Moon had worshiped. The pastor spoke to us through an interpreter, and then some of the members sang hymns. When they finished, our group stood and sang through choked voices and tear-filled eyes.

As we left the church, we passed a monument erected to remember Lottie Moon's ministry to and love for the Chinese people. The monument testified to the perseverance of the Christian faith and God's love through the years and despite adversity.

Christ's birth, life, death, and resurrection motivated Lottie Moon to travel halfway around the world to help bring the gospel to China. She invested her life in ministering to the Chinese people, sharing her faith, and raising awareness and support for missions. She honored the Savior's birth.

Thousands before and after Lottie Moon have honored the Savior's birth through ministry to others. Some have journeyed to distant nations to spread the gospel and minister. Others have stayed in their home nations where they have shared the good news and spread God's love. We stand in the long line of these servants of God. Studying Matthew's account of Jesus' birth enables us to see how Joseph and the wise men honored Jesus' birth and encourages us to honor our Savior's birth by living for Him and sharing the gospel.

Matthew 1:18–2:12
1. Heeding the Angel's Message (Matt. 1:18-25)
2. Seeking the King (Matt. 2:1-8)
3. Honoring the Savior (Matt. 2:9-12)

THE BACKGROUND

During the time of Joseph and Mary's betrothal, Joseph discovered Mary had become pregnant. Being a righteous individual, Joseph decided to divorce Mary whom he believed had been unfaithful to him. Being a kind individual, Joseph decided to divorce Mary quietly to spare her additional embarrassment. While Joseph was deciding how to proceed with the divorce, an angel appeared to him in a dream. The angel explained that Mary's pregnancy resulted from the action of the Holy Spirit and not from unfaithfulness. The angel stated Mary would give birth to a special Son who would bear the name Jesus and provide salvation from sin. Matthew quoted Isaiah 7:14 to indicate Jesus' birth would fulfill Old Testament prophecy. Knowing the true source of Mary's Child, Joseph married her but did not have sexual relations with her until after the Son's birth. Joseph named the Child Jesus as the angel had instructed (Matt. 1:18-25).

After Jesus' birth in Bethlehem during the reign of Herod the Great, wise men saw an unusual star. They interpreted the star as announcing the birth of a new King of the Jews and journeyed to Jerusalem to find and worship the King. The wise men's news troubled Herod and others. Herod assembled the chief priests and scribes to determine where Scripture stated the Messiah would be born. Quoting Micah 5:2, they informed Herod that Bethlehem would be the Messiah's birthplace. Herod instructed the wise men to find Jesus and return to give him the Child's location (Matt. 2:1-8).

The wise men followed the star and arrived in Bethlehem, where they found Jesus in a house with Mary, His mother. They worshiped Jesus and gave Him gifts suitable for a king. After God warned them in a dream of Herod's true intent, the wise men went home by a different route (2:9-12).

THE BIBLE PASSAGE

1. Heeding the Angel's Message (Matt. 1:18-25)

Verse 18: The birth of Jesus Christ came about this way: After His mother Mary had been engaged to Joseph, it was discovered before they came together that she was pregnant by the Holy Spirit.

Having provided Jesus' genealogy, revealing His lineage through Abraham and David, Matthew described Jesus' birth. Mary and Joseph were **engaged** or betrothed when Mary became pregnant with Jesus. First-century Jewish marriage customs differed from ours. Parents typically arranged a marriage and the parents, man, and woman entered into a binding agreement before witnesses. Usually the woman would be 12 or 13 years old at the time of the engagement and the man would be older. The man and woman did not live together or have sexual relations during the time of engagement, but the community considered them husband and wife. If the man died, the community referred to the woman as a widow. If the woman died, the community understood the man to be a widower. If the woman had sexual relations with another man, she was guilty of adultery against her husband. Usually a year after the engagement or betrothal, a public marriage ceremony occurred, and the man took his bride into his home.

During the betrothal Mary became **pregnant**, but not from sexual relations with a man. The Holy Spirit caused her to conceive a very special Child. Old Testament writers referred to the active role of God's Spirit in the creation of the world (Gen. 1:2) and in the re-creation of God's people following the Babylonian exile (Ezek. 37:9-10,14). Rabbis also expected the Holy Spirit to be actively involved when the Messiah arrived to renew Israel.

Matthew did not explain how the Holy Spirit worked in Mary's life to conceive Jesus. We live in a time accustomed to medical diagnoses and explanations. Yet we continue to live in a world where not everything can be explained medically or scientifically. In an inexplicable, miraculous way, God worked in a young woman's life to bring His Son into the world to accomplish His saving purpose.

Verse 19: **So her husband Joseph, being a righteous man, and not wanting to disgrace her publicly, decided to divorce her secretly.**

Unaware of the Holy Spirit's involvement in Mary's pregnancy, Joseph assumed Mary had been unfaithful to him. The marriage relationship comprised an important part of Jewish social order, and Mary's pregnancy indicated a disregard for the community's and God's law. As a **righteous man**, Joseph knew he could not marry a woman who ignored God's laws. He determined **to divorce her**.

Joseph's love for Mary led him to plan to divorce her **secretly** so as not to **disgrace her publicly**. Joseph's commitment to obey the law was tempered with compassion. A public divorce would lead to humiliation before the community and trial as an adulteress. Joseph decided to take another option that allowed him to end the marriage agreement before two witnesses. If the elders found Mary guilty of adultery, she faced the death penalty. Joseph sought to act redemptively and compassionately while still obeying the law.

Verse 20: **But after he had considered these things, an angel of the Lord suddenly appeared to him in a dream, saying, "Joseph, son of David, don't be afraid to take Mary as your wife, because what has been conceived in her is by the Holy Spirit.**

As Joseph considered his course of action, God sent an angel to speak to him in a dream. In the Old Testament dreams and angels constituted important methods God used to communicate with individuals. Matthew noted God's continued use of dreams to communicate with the wise men (Matt. 2:12), Joseph (2:13,19-20,22), and Pilate's wife (27:19).

The angel instructed Joseph to marry Mary. She had not been unfaithful to him. Rather than being unfaithful, God had found Mary to be so faithful, He had selected her to bear His Son (see Luke 1:26-38). The angel reminded Joseph of his status as a **son of David**. If Joseph married Mary, the community would understand Joseph as Jesus' legal father. Thus Jesus, the Messiah, would be a descendant of David as prophesied (Isa. 11:1; Jer. 23:5).

Verse 21: **She will give birth to a son, and you are to name Him Jesus, because He will save His people from their sins."**

The angel stated Mary would deliver a Son and instructed Joseph to name Him **Jesus**. The name *Jesus* is the Greek form of the Hebrew name "Joshua." The name meant "the Lord is salvation" and served as a common name among Jews in the first century A.D. Since people in the ancient world understood a name as indicating the character and destiny of the individual, many parents might have given their son the name *Jesus* with the hope that God might use that son to free their land from Roman rule or that at least during the son's life, God would act to save His people. The angel said the name *Jesus* would describe Jesus' role not as a military deliverer but as One who would **save His people from their sins**. While many in Israel hoped for political independence, salvation from sin constituted their deepest need (see Jer. 31:31-34). Through Jesus God would provide salvation from sin for all who would believe in Him.

Verse 22: **Now all this took place to fulfill what was spoken by the Lord through the prophet:**

Matthew often indicated that events in Jesus' life fulfilled Old Testament prophecy (for example, see Matt. 2:15,23; 8:17; 27:9-10). By doing so, he emphasized three things. First, Matthew indicated God had been preparing for Jesus' coming for centuries by sending prophets to point out Israel's need and God's solution. Second, the Old Testament prophecies fulfilled in Jesus proved Jesus was the Messiah for which Israel had been waiting. Third, God's fulfillment of Old Testament prophecies in Jesus demonstrated God's continued faithfulness to each new generation.

Verse 23: **See, the virgin will become pregnant and give birth to a son, and they will name Him Immanuel, which is translated "God is with us."**

This verse records the first quotation of Old Testament prophecy in Matthew's Gospel. Under divine inspiration he recognized that Jesus' birth fulfilled the prophecy of Isaiah 7:14. The name **Immanuel,** meaning "God with us," looked toward One who would uniquely represent God in His Person. Mary conceived Jesus by the power of the Holy Spirit, and the title *Immanuel,* "God with us," accurately described Jesus' identity and mission (see Matt. 28:20).

The angel's explanation would have been as difficult for Joseph to comprehend in his time as for us to understand in our time. As humans, we typically look for logical, reasonable explanations to events before considering God's miraculous involvement. Joseph had initially understood Mary's pregnancy as resulting from her unfaithfulness. When God told Joseph He had done something unique in Mary, Joseph believed God and honored Him by trusting Him. When God speaks to us through the Bible, the Holy Spirit, or His servants, we honor God by believing His message.

Verse 24: When Joseph got up from sleeping, he did as the Lord's angel had commanded him. He married her

Joseph followed his belief with action. When Joseph awakened, **he did as the Lord's angel had commanded him**. The angel's words must have agreed with what Joseph already knew of Mary and her godly character. More importantly, the righteous Joseph heard God's voice and purpose in the angel's words. Joseph obeyed God by marrying Mary and taking her into his home.

When Joseph believed the angel's words and acted on them, he honored God. To believe in God, in Christ, or in a church doctrine and not act on that belief does not honor God. Faith evidences itself in a life transformed by a personal relationship with God. Celebrating Christmas with manger scenes, pageants, choral programs, and worship services and then living as if Christ has not been born does not honor God. Like Joseph, let us hear God and respond in obedience. •

Verse 25: but did not know her intimately until she gave birth to a son. And he named Him Jesus.

Joseph married Mary **but did not know her intimately until she gave birth to a son**. The word *until* strongly implies that following the birth of Jesus, Joseph and Mary enjoyed sexual relations like any normal married couple (see Matt. 12:46).

People surely gossiped when Joseph honored his marriage covenant with Mary. Undoubtedly they whispered unkind and untrue words about Mary's supposed unfaithfulness. Perhaps they even confronted Joseph and Mary about what they viewed as "immorality." Such gossip probably haunted the family for years. Yet having believed God's explanation of Mary's pregnancy, Joseph obeyed God by marrying her and braving misunderstanding and criticism.

Obeying God sometimes causes us to act in ways that may be misunderstood or criticized by others. When we forgive others, some will see our forgiveness as a sign of weakness. When we try to give others another chance, some will see us as gullible. When we refuse to engage in gossip, some will see us as pretending to be better than they are. We honor God by obeying Him and patiently bearing the misunderstanding and criticism we receive as a result of that obedience.

FOR FURTHER STUDY

In what situations have people misunderstood your motives or actions as you lived the Christian life?

2. Seeking the King (Matt. 2:1-8)

Verse 1: **After Jesus was born in Bethlehem of Judea in the days of King Herod, wise men from the east arrived unexpectedly in Jerusalem,**

The town of Bethlehem, whose name means "house of bread," lay about five miles south of Jerusalem. Bethlehem served as David's hometown and there Samuel found and anointed him as Israel's king (1 Sam. 16:1). Since the Messiah was to come from King David's line, Bethlehem constituted the ideal place for Jesus to be born.

Herod the Great ruled over the Jews and under the auspices of Rome from 37 to 4 B.C. Herod's father, Antipater, who served as governor of biblical Palestine under Rome, helped Herod become governor of Galilee. Herod used his political skills to eventually become ruler over Judea as well. Antipater came from Idumea, an area also known as Edom, located southeast of the Dead Sea. During the time of Jewish independence (167-63 B.C.), the Jews forced the Idumeans either to convert to Judaism or to leave the area. Herod's association with Rome and his Idumean ancestry made him an unacceptable king to many Jews.

Although Herod engaged in various building projects, such as the remodeling of the Jerusalem temple, and fed the people through royal charity during a time of famine, he placed a heavy tax burden on the Jews, drafted many into forced labor, and became increasingly paranoid that he might lose his throne and life in a coup. To protect himself he killed those around him who might pose a threat to his power. These individuals included his wife Mariamne and some of his sons. The Roman Senate appointed Herod king of the Jews, a title fitting his political status but not his commitment to his subjects. Since Herod the Great died in 4 B.C., most Bible scholars date Jesus' birth to approximately 6 B.C.

The **wise men from the east** may have come from Babylon or Persia. While not kings, these wise men possessed both political and religious power. People believed the wise men's observation of stars and planets provided them with special insight regarding world and national affairs. Their unexpected arrival in Jerusalem would have caused interest.

Verse 2: saying, "Where is He who has been born King of the Jews? For we saw His star in the east and have come to worship Him."

Upon arriving in Jerusalem, the wise men stated the purpose of their visit. They had come seeking the newly born **King of the Jews**. They reported a star had appeared in the sky in their eastern homeland and they had interpreted the star as announcing the birth of a special King for the Jews. Assuming the new King would have been born into the current royal family, the wise men came to Jerusalem to find him and **worship Him**.

Some Bible scholars have tried to identify the star as a conjunction of planets, a comet, or a supernova. While God certainly could have used natural phenomena in indicating Jesus' birth, the star constituted a miraculous phenomenon created by God specifically to announce the birth of His Son. God used the unique creation of a special star to announce the unique event of the birth of His Son.

Verse 3: When King Herod heard this, he was deeply disturbed, and all Jerusalem with him.

The wise men apparently did not present themselves to Herod (see Matt. 2:7), but Herod soon discovered their mission. The wise men had responded with joy and enthusiasm to the message of the star and set out to find the King. When Herod learned of their mission, he responded by being **deeply disturbed**. Herod knew his Idumean ancestry made him vulnerable to a coup by the Jews. He feared and disposed of any rival. News of the birth of one who might try to dethrone him would have greatly disturbed him. The idea of respect being paid to another as "King of the Jews" also would have angered Herod. The Roman Senate had given him that title, and he carefully guarded it.

The wise men's mission also disturbed **all Jerusalem**. Some Bible students believe *all Jerusalem* referred primarily to the religious leaders. Since Herod had appointed many of them, anything that disturbed Herod would also disturb them. Other Bible scholars suggest *all Jerusalem* referred to everyone living in the city. Knowing Herod's paranoia and cruelty, they feared what Herod might do in response to the wise men's quest.

Verse 4: So he assembled all the chief priests and scribes of the people and asked them where the Messiah would be born.

Though Herod was part-Jew as well as part-Idumean, he did not know **where the Messiah would be born**. To find out, he summoned the religious leaders. The **chief priests** included the priests who directed the 24 orders of priests who lived in and around Jerusalem. The **scribes** referred to the group of scholars who copied, interpreted, and applied the Old Testament. These scholars stood in the long line of individuals who continued Ezra's ministry. Herod knew exactly whom to call to discover where the threat to his power might be.

Verse 5a: "In Bethlehem of Judea," they told him,

The chief priests and scribes told Herod the Messiah would be born in **Bethlehem of Judea**. The tribal area of Zebulun also contained a town named Bethlehem located about seven miles northwest of Nazareth (Josh. 19:15). As David's hometown and the place where Samuel anointed David king, Bethlehem of Judah had a richer history. In addition, Bethlehem lay only five miles from Jerusalem. This fact made the news of the birth of a king a greater threat from Herod's perspective.

Prophecy supported Bethlehem of Judea as the Messiah's birthplace. The chief priests and scribes referred Herod to Micah 5:2-4, a messianic passage that indicated God would raise up a ruler from Bethlehem who would shepherd His people and whose greatness would extend to the earth's ends. The earthly kings of Israel typically failed to lead the people in godly paths, and the greatness of the kings rarely extended beyond biblical Palestine. In Bethlehem a king would be born who would do what Israel's kings had not done. God's Messiah would reveal God's compassion and love to all people and create a kingdom that knew no physical or temporal bounds.

Herod secretly summoned the wise men to discover exactly when they had first seen the star. Undoubtedly he had sent the chief priests and scribes away before calling for the wise men. The chief priests and scribes might have welcomed the news of a new, great king being born who would take Herod's place and might have warned the wise men not to trust Herod. Herod then sent the wise men to Bethlehem. He encouraged them to find the Child and then report back to him so he also could go and worship. Later the wise men received a warning through a dream that revealed the true character and intent of Herod (Matt. 2:12).

The response of Herod to news of the special birth contrasted sharply with the wise men's response. Herod responded in fear. He desired to remove any threat to his power. The wise men responded with joy. They made a long journey to find the Child and worship Him. Jesus' birth would impact the entire world by bringing God's offer of salvation to all people. As Jesus' earthly life began, Gentiles responded with interest and excitement to His birth, while the Judean king and others in the royal court and city became deeply disturbed and distressed.

Some today still see Jesus as a threat and thus do not seek Him. For them Jesus demands too much when He asks to be Lord of their lives. They do not want to relinquish control. They and we need to see Jesus not as a threat to our independence but as a Savior who through His life, death, and resurrection enabled and empowered us to live a fulfilling life under His guidance and lordship. As the wise men sought Jesus to worship Him, we need to seek Him daily to follow Him.

3. Honoring the Savior (Matt. 2:9-12)

Verse 9: **After hearing the king, they went on their way. And there it was—the star they had seen in the east! It led them until it came and stopped above the place where the child was.**

After the wise men's audience with Herod, they left for Bethlehem. As they looked in the direction of Bethlehem, they again saw the star they had first seen while observing the night sky in Babylon or Persia. The star that had first drawn their attention **led them** to the precise spot in Bethlehem where Jesus lived with Mary and Joseph. The movement of the star makes the interpretation of the star as a natural astronomical phenomenon difficult to sustain. A conjunction of planets, a comet, or a supernova would have captured the attention of the wise men, but none of the natural phenomena would have moved through the night sky leading the wise men five miles to the exact location of Jesus.

Verse 10: **When they saw the star, they were overjoyed beyond measure.**

The appearance of the star filled the wise men with great joy. When they first saw the star, they believed it brought a divine message concerning the birth of a great King in Israel. Their journey had led them far from their home over a great distance. They probably interpreted their safe journey as resulting from divine guidance and protection. As they neared the end of their quest to find and worship the newborn King, they marveled joyfully that the star continued to guide them.

Verse 11: **Entering the house, they saw the child with Mary His mother, and falling to their knees, they worshiped Him. Then they opened their treasures and presented Him with gifts: gold, frankincense, and myrrh.**

The star pointed the way to the **house** where Jesus, Mary, and Joseph lived. The mention of the house and the age limit of the children Herod later ordered killed in Bethlehem (Matt. 2:16) indicate a significant amount of time had passed since Jesus' birth. Mary, Joseph, and Jesus had left the stable where Mary gave birth to Jesus (Luke 2:7) and settled in a house as residents of Bethlehem. A careful examination of verses 7 and 16 of Matthew 2 suggest that a lapse of between one and two years had occurred since Jesus was born.

When the wise men saw Jesus, they fell **to their knees** and **worshiped Him**. In the ancient world falling to one's knees and prostrating oneself facedown before an individual represented respect for and submission to the person. When we worship God, we acknowledge His power and authority over the world and over us. Knowing God, His love, and His greatness leads to praising Him and committing ourselves to obey and serve Him.

The lavish gifts the wise men brought also demonstrated their recognition of and submission to the Lord. The Old Testament looked to a time when the nations would bring expensive gifts to Israel's king in recognition of his sovereignty (Ps. 72:10-11,15; Isa. 60:6). The wise men's worship of and gifts to Jesus fulfilled such prophecies.

The wise men presented Jesus with **gold, frankincense, and myrrh**, all gifts suitable for royalty. Throughout all time people have valued gold as a precious, valuable metal that only the wealthy or powerful possessed in any quantity. Certain balsam trees produced frankincense, a resinous substance from which people made perfume. People often used incense, like frankincense, in worship. Myrrh was a fragrant, resinous substance used in preparing anointing oil, in making people and clothes smell good, and in embalming bodies. Some Bible scholars interpret each gift as indicating something about Jesus. The gold emphasized His royalty, the frankincense His divinity, and the myrrh His coming death and burial. While we may see the gifts as representing various characteristics of and the destiny of Jesus, the wise men primarily gave the best gifts they could to honor the newborn King. The three gifts led to the traditional belief that three wise men came to visit Jesus. Matthew did not provide the exact number of wise men.

The New Testament does not reveal what Mary and Joseph did with the gifts. Some Bible scholars suggest they sold them to travel to and live in Egypt. Rather than wondering what happened to the gifts, we need to share the wonder and worship of the wise men as they knelt before Jesus.

God warned the wise men not to report to Herod regarding Jesus' location. They obeyed and returned to their home by an alternate route.

In this Christmas season, we can honor Christ in at least two ways. If we have never accepted Christ as Savior, we can honor His birth by accepting Him. If we have accepted Christ, we can rededicate ourselves to living daily for Him and leading others to faith in Him. Part of following Christ involves giving generously of our financial resources, time, and talents. As we honor those we love by giving gifts, we can honor God by giving ourselves.

FOR FURTHER STUDY

What do you find most amazing about the wise men coming to worship Jesus? How does that fact indicate the wonder of Jesus' birth? List three things you will do this Christmas season to show Jesus is Lord of your life.

The Week of December 31

WORKING COOPERATIVELY

Background Passage: Nehemiah 1:1–3:32
Lesson Passages: Nehemiah 1:1-4,11; 2:4-5,8b,17-18; 3:1-2

INTRODUCTION

"I propose we begin a new mission in the south side of town," stated Julie. "I have been praying about this possibility for the last six months and believe God has called us to minister to those people. Who is with me?"

Several enthusiastic voices answered. "Amen, Julie," said Bill. "I'm not very good at teaching, but I will be happy to help with the organization of the mission. We will need a place to meet and a schedule of volunteers."

"Well, I will be happy to teach," responded Fred. "Do we need someone also to organize some activities to introduce ourselves to the community?"

"I would enjoy doing that," answered Megan. "Some of the activities we did in college for Baptist Student Union would work."

"Looks like we have a talented and dedicated group," said the pastor. "Let's plan to meet this Sunday afternoon. In the meantime, I ask everyone to pray daily for this new ministry. God can accomplish so much through our cooperative work!"

Most projects in life require cooperation between people with different talents. Architects, electricians, plumbers, carpenters, masons, and others work cooperatively to construct a building. Pilots, flight attendants, mechanics, accountants, administrators, and others work together to operate an airline. Faculty, staff, administration, and students create an educational institution.

Ministry also necessitates cooperation. No one can or needs to do everything. Each church has people with different interests and abilities. By working cooperatively they can accomplish great things with God's power. When Nehemiah led the people in Judah to rebuild the wall, he demonstrated how God can use cooperation to accomplish His will and bless His people.

Nehemiah 1:1–3:32
1. Heartbreaking News (Neh. 1:1-11)
2. Building Plans (Neh. 2:1-20)
3. Reporting Progress (Neh. 3:1-32)

THE BACKGROUND

In the 20th year of Artaxerxes I, Nehemiah, the king's cupbearer, heard of the condition of Jerusalem and its inhabitants. He responded with grief and prayer. In his daily prayers, he praised God and confessed his and his people's sins. He also referred to the teachings of Deuteronomy that promised punishment for sin but restoration for obedience. Nehemiah asked God to show compassion to His people and restore them (Neh. 1:1-11).

Four months after Nehemiah had learned about the terrible condition of Jerusalem, God gave him the opportunity to approach Artaxerxes with his concern. Nehemiah told the king about the disrepair of Jerusalem and asked Artaxerxes to allow him to go to Jerusalem and lead in the rebuilding. After discussion the king agreed. Nehemiah requested letters from the king for safe passage and to secure wood for the rebuilding.

Nehemiah received the letters, made the journey, and delivered the letters to the appropriate individuals. Two leaders, Sanballat and Tobiah, in the area of biblical Palestine quickly expressed their displeasure at Nehemiah's presence and plan. During the night Nehemiah inspected Jerusalem's wall. He then spoke to the officials and others and gathered support for the rebuilding. Sanballat, Tobiah, and Geshem tried to stop the rebuilding, but Nehemiah responded with confidence in God. He disputed their claim to the city (2:1-20).

Nehemiah recruited a variety of people to help with the rebuilding of Jerusalem's walls. While some refused to participate, priests, goldsmiths, merchants, and others joined in the effort. The walls began to rise again under the cooperative work of the people (3:1-32).

THE BIBLE PASSAGE

1. Heartbreaking News (Neh. 1:1-11)

Verse 1: **The words of Nehemiah son of Hacaliah: During the month of Chislev in the twentieth year, when I was in the fortress city of Susa,**

The work of Nehemiah and Ezra overlapped. Nehemiah's name means "the Lord comforts or encourages," and he lived up to his name by bringing comfort and hope to the people of Jerusalem and Judah. He served as their governor, led in the rebuilding of the city walls, and helped the people follow God more closely.

The mention of the **twentieth year** without giving a reference point has resulted in a difference of opinion among Bible scholars. Some have suggested the phrase refers to Nehemiah's 20th year in the king's service, but that seems unlikely. Most scholars believe Nehemiah referred to the 20th year of the reign of Artaxerxes I, the king Nehemiah served as cupbearer.

Like Ezra, Nehemiah dated events by the year of the reigning king (for example, Ezra 1:1; 7:7).

Artaxerxes's 20th year would have been 445 B.C. Artaxerxes I began his reign in 464 B.C. and immediately faced a rebellion from his brother Hystaspes [hih STAHS peez]. No sooner did Artaxerxes quell that rebellion than revolt broke out in Egypt in 460 B.C. The Athenians supported the Egyptian revolt, but Artaxerxes finally crushed the rebellion in 455 B.C. In 448 B.C. Megabyzus, the satrap of the Trans-Euphrates province, rebelled but later became reconciled to the king. Maintaining control and loyalty in Judah would have constituted a priority for Artaxerxes.

The month of Chislev [KISS Lehv] spanned from late November through early December. Susa [SOO suh] was the Persian royal winter residence and administrative capital. Artaxerxes spent much of his time in Susa, which was located in modern Iran. The mention of Nehemiah living in Susa provided an early indication that Nehemiah served in the royal court.

Verse 2: Hanani, one of my brothers, arrived with men from Judah, and I questioned them about Jerusalem and the Jewish remnant that had returned from exile.

The use of the phrase **one of my brothers** to describe Hanani [huh NAY nigh] could identify Hanani as Nehemiah's sibling, as Nehemiah's relative, or simply as a Jew. Since Nehemiah again called him "my brother" when he later placed Hanani in charge of Jerusalem, Nehemiah and Hanani probably were actual brothers (Neh. 7:2). The name **Hanani** means "the Lord has been gracious."

Bible scholars have differing opinions regarding the relationship of Hanani to the **men from Judah**. Some suggest Hanani lived near Jerusalem and had recently returned to tell his brother of the difficult conditions in Jerusalem with the hope that Nehemiah could intercede with Artaxerxes. Nehemiah's grief-stricken response to the conditions in Jerusalem and Judah would certainly make sense if he knew his brother lived under such conditions. Others think Hanani lived in Persia but had recently been to Judah on a fact-finding mission and had returned to report to Nehemiah. Probably the group came to Hanani in Susa and asked him to introduce them to Nehemiah so they might report and encourage his intercession with the king.

Hanani and Nehemiah both shared a deep concern for those in Jerusalem and Judah. When Hanani heard the report from the men, he knew Nehemiah would also want to hear. Knowing Artaxerxes had earlier stopped the rebuilding of Jerusalem's walls (Ezra 4:8-23), both Hanani and Nehemiah understood and grieved regarding the condition of Judah and the Jews.

Verse 3: They said to me, "The survivors in the province, who returned from the exile, are in great trouble and disgrace. Jerusalem's wall has been broken down, and its gates have been burned down."

Although the delegation from Judah focused on those **who returned from the exile,** their report referred to the conditions of all who lived in Judah. While some Bible scholars believe the **province** referred to Judah or Samaria, most Bible scholars believe *province* refers to the large Trans-Euphrates area administered by a satrap. Judah comprised a very small part of a huge empire, but Hanani, Nehemiah, and God cared deeply for the people of Judah.

The delegation brought a disheartening report. The people of Judah lived in **great trouble and disgrace** resulting from the humiliation they had experienced through the Babylonian army's destruction of Jerusalem and the frustrations created by their inability to rebuild Jerusalem's walls. Over a hundred years after Jerusalem's destruction the walls remained **broken down** and the gates **burned down.** Exiles had returned with great hopes but little had been accomplished. Life remained hard and the people continued to be discouraged.

Bible scholars disagree as to whether the conditions resulted from Nebuchadnezzar's destruction of Jerusalem in 587 B.C. or later destruction. None of those who lived in Judah would have remembered the destruction of Jerusalem by Nebuchadnezzar's army although they could still see the effects of that destruction. Probably the destruction of 587 B.C. had been supplemented in recent years by enemies destroying portions of the wall the people of Judah had managed to rebuild. Perhaps when Artaxerxes commanded the rebuilding of the walls to cease, enemies of the Jews tore down what the Jews had rebuilt.

Verse 4: When I heard these words, I sat down and wept. I mourned for a number of days, fasting and praying before the God of heaven.

Many in America try to restrain their feelings in times of grief so as not to appear weak, but other cultures express their grief with passion. In the ancient world weeping and fasting formed a typical response to terrible news (for example, Ezra 9:3-4; 10:6). When Nehemiah heard the news brought by the delegation from Judah, he **sat down and wept.** For an extended period, he fasted and prayed. He poured out his feelings to God. Jerusalem's condition devastated Nehemiah. He realized the lack of strong defenses made Jerusalem and Judah vulnerable to enemies, and the despair of the people jeopardized their witness to God. As he grieved for Jerusalem and the Jews, he asked God to intervene.

Nehemiah's beautiful prayer began by praising God and invoking His presence (Neh. 1:5-6a). Nehemiah used the term "God of heaven" as descriptive of the One true God who dwelled in heaven and accomplished

His will on earth (see Gen. 24:7). "LORD" or *Yahweh* translated God's name revealed to Moses (Ex. 3:14-15). Nehemiah's description of God as "great and awe-inspiring" echoed Deuteronomy (Deut. 7:21). Nehemiah's request to God to listen to his prayer did not imply Nehemiah believed he had to do something extreme to get God's attention. Nehemiah knew God heard his prayer. He was asking God to act in response to his prayer and restore Judah.

Following his invocation of God, Nehemiah confessed his and his people's sins (Neh. 1:6b-7). Nehemiah did not exclude himself. His prayer reveals that he did not view himself as innocent, while everyone else was guilty. He identified with his people because like them he also had sinned. Nehemiah confessed his and the Israelites' sins as failure to keep God's law. They had sinned not out of ignorance but out of willful disobedience.

Nehemiah stated God had warned Israel not to disobey (Deut. 4:25-27), but Israel had rebelled. As a result God had justly punished His people with exile (Neh. 1:8). Nehemiah asked God to remember His people and how He delivered them in the past and act to give them a new future (1:9-10).

Verse 11: Please, Lord, let Your ear be attentive to the prayer of Your servant and to that of Your servants who delight to revere Your name. Give Your servant success today, and have compassion on him in the presence of this man.

⌊At the time,⌋ **I was the king's cupbearer.**

Nehemiah again appealed to God to act on behalf of His people. Babylonian conquest had destroyed Jerusalem. The return from exile had not resulted in the new Israel the people had expected. Artaxerxes, the reigning Persian king, had continued policies designed to keep Judah weak. Each day Nehemiah asked God to have compassion on His people and give him **success today**. Nehemiah prayed that when God provided him the opportunity to approach Artaxerxes about the situation in Judah, he would be ready to follow God and help his people. Nehemiah maintained a constant trust and hope in God. He was confident God would answer His prayer and act to restore His people.

Nehemiah referred to Artaxerxes as **this man**. Although Artaxerxes wielded absolute power over Persia, in God's eyes he was simply another human being, created and loved by God but having no power or authority to rival God. Nehemiah realized neither he nor any other persons could cause Artaxerxes to reverse his previous policy and allow the rebuilding of Jerusalem's wall. Only God could effect that change. Nehemiah praised and appealed to the only One who could deliver Judah.

Long before Nehemiah prayed and asked God's help, God had been preparing him to lead His people. Nehemiah held the position of **king's cupbearer**. The cupbearer selected and served the king's wine, always tasting the wine first to ensure no one had poisoned the wine in an attempt to kill the king. The cupbearer enjoyed access to and influence with the king. He occupied a high-ranking position. God had brought Nehemiah to the position of cupbearer for a reason. God the Heavenly King would answer Nehemiah's prayer through Nehemiah's position as a trusted servant of an earthly king.

When Nehemiah learned of the terrible condition of his people, he prayed for God's intervention and offered himself as a means through which God could accomplish His will. We all need to pray like Nehemiah and ask God to give us the courage, compassion, and dedication to act when He provides the opportunity. Prayer often creates changes in the world by first creating changes within us. By making ourselves available to God, God can bless us and others.

FOR FURTHER STUDY

Read Deuteronomy 30:1-10. How does Scripture help us know better how to pray?

2. Building Plans (Neh. 2:1-20)

The mention of the month of Nisan (late March, early April) indicated four months had passed since Nehemiah first learned of the desperate situation in Jerusalem. Throughout the four months he had engaged in an attitude of intense prayer and planning. He ably performed his duties as cupbearer but the problems of Jerusalem and Judah remained uppermost in his thoughts or prayers. Probably during this time as Nehemiah prayed, he sensed God's call to go to Judah and allow God to use him in restoring His people.

As Nehemiah served Artaxerxes, the king noticed his sadness, an emotion Nehemiah had never previously demonstrated in the king's presence. Expressing concern and sensitivity, the king diagnosed Nehemiah's sadness as resulting from grief rather than illness.

Some Bible scholars suggest that since Nisan served as the first month of the Persian year, Artaxerxes and the Persians were celebrating a new year's feast. Perhaps during the feast the king demonstrated special generosity to his subjects, and thus Nehemiah chose this occasion to allow the king to see the grief he had kept hidden the past four months. Yet despite the perhaps opportune time, Nehemiah still took a risk and feared the king's possible reaction. Three concerns may have contributed to Nehemiah's fear. First, seeing Nehemiah's emotional state might have made the king suspicious of a plot against him that involved Nehemiah. Second, Artaxerxes might have become angry with Nehemiah's sadness during a festive occasion. Third, Nehemiah may have been filled with anxiety regarding Artaxerxes's response to his request. After suspending construction of Jerusalem's wall in the past, would Artaxerxes allow him to go and complete the rebuilding?

Despite his fear Nehemiah answered the king politely and passionately. He informed Artaxerxes of the ruined condition of his ancestral home and emphasized his connection with the city. His ancestors lay buried in a city that lay in ruins.

Verse 4: **Then the king asked me, "What is your request?" So I prayed to the God of heaven**

Artaxerxes's answer must have somewhat soothed Nehemiah's fear. Evidently Artaxerxes held a deep respect and appreciation for Nehemiah and wanted to help him. God had prepared the way for Nehemiah to make his request.

Probably Nehemiah's brief, silent prayer summarized his prayers of the past four months and asked God to bring success to his request. Many of us have offered quick prayers when faced with a situation for which we had not adequately prepared. Students pray before taking a test for which they have not studied. Employees pray before entering a suddenly-called meeting with a supervisor. Nehemiah's brief prayer followed months of praying and planning. He had requested God's help and guidance, prepared for this meeting, and then asked God to bring his prayers to fruition.

Verse 5: **and answered the king, "If it pleases the king, and if your servant has found favor with you, send me to Judah and to the city where my ancestors are buried, so that I may rebuild it."**

Nehemiah addressed Artaxerxes according to court etiquette. Although Artaxerxes did not share Nehemiah's faith, the king held a position of authority over Nehemiah and deserved proper respect. Nehemiah asked Artaxerxes to allow him to return to Judah and rebuild the city where his ancestors lay buried.

Artaxerxes asked Nehemiah two questions that indicated his desire not to lose Nehemiah's services as his cupbearer. The king wanted to know how long Nehemiah would be gone and when he would return. Nehemiah answered the king's questions satisfactorily, and the king granted him permission to go and rebuild. Nehemiah also requested letters of introduction to the governors he would encounter along the way in order to guarantee that he would have safe passage to Judah. He further requested a letter to present to Asaph who managed the king's forest so Nehemiah could secure wood for rebuilding the fortress gates, the city wall, and a residence for himself (Neh. 2:6-8a).

Verse 8b: **The king granted my ⌊requests⌋, for I was graciously strengthened by my God.**

Nehemiah attributed Artaxerxes's granting of his requests to God's intervention. No amount of planning or scheming could have caused Artaxerxes to reverse his previous decree to stop the rebuilding of Jerusalem's wall (see Ezra 4:17-22). Only God could have changed Artaxerxes's heart to allow Nehemiah to travel to Judah and supervise the rebuilding. Like a good leader, Nehemiah not only prayed and planned, he also trusted God to provide the opportunity and means to a successful conclusion.

Nehemiah maintained a constant attitude of prayer and developed plans for approaching the king and helping his people. When God presented the opportunity, Nehemiah boldly acted. Prayer needs to lead us to confident action as well. Like Nehemiah we need to maintain an attitude of constant prayer, prepare as well as possible, and act when God provides the opportunity so we may serve Him effectively.

FOR FURTHER STUDY
How does research and planning help us serve God better?

As soon as practical, Nehemiah left for Judah. Although Ezra had refused a military escort (Ezra 8:22), the presence of a military escort for Nehemiah did not indicate a lack of faith on his part. Artaxerxes sent a military escort with Nehemiah probably to protect his cupbearer on his mission. Nehemiah's arrival created immediate problems with the neighboring governors and demonstrated the wisdom of the military escort. Sanballat served as governor of Samaria and Tobiah as governor of Ammon (Neh. 2:9-10). No doubt they viewed Nehemiah's presence as a threat to their power and influence.

After a three-day rest, Nehemiah took a few men with him and conducted a night survey of Jerusalem's walls (2:11-12). Before organizing the rebuilding effort, he needed to determine the extent of the damage. No doubt he continued to pray as he conducted his research.

The piles of rubble around Jerusalem made a complete circuit of the city impossible. Nehemiah returned without Jerusalem's officials knowing what he had done or planned to do (Neh. 2:13-16). Again Nehemiah demonstrated the careful research characteristic of good leaders.

Verse 17: **So I said to them, "You see the trouble we are in. Jerusalem lies in ruins and its gates have been burned down. Come, let's rebuild Jerusalem's wall, so that we will no longer be a disgrace."**

Following the inspection of Jerusalem's wall, Nehemiah called the people of Jerusalem together to tell them why he had come. He summarized the condition of the city using almost the same words the delegation from Judah had used when they reported to him (1:3). Nehemiah identified himself as an inhabitant of Jerusalem. Even in Susa he had considered

Jerusalem his city. After arriving in Jerusalem he felt a deeper connection to the city and its people.

Nehemiah invited the people to **rebuild Jerusalem's wall** and thus eliminate their **disgrace**. Part of Judah's disgrace lay in Jerusalem's vulnerability because an unwalled city was at the mercy of its enemies. For Nehemiah the ruined condition of Jerusalem reflected badly on the Jews' commitment to God and constituted a greater disgrace. The people had grown to accept their current situation as normal. Nehemiah sought to stir their faith in God and make them and the city a witness to God's power and glory.

Verse 18: I told them how the gracious hand of my God had been on me, and what the king had said to me.

They said, "Let's start rebuilding," and they were encouraged to ⌊do⌋ this good work.

Nehemiah gave the people reason to believe they could accomplish the rebuilding. He noted how gracious God had been to him. God had changed his mind so the king who at one time had opposed the rebuilding had sent Nehemiah to accomplish the rebuilding. Nehemiah believed his very presence in Jerusalem under the auspices of the king testified to God's miraculous intervention for His people.

The people's enthusiastic, positive response to Nehemiah's call to action indicated God's gracious hand continued to act. Nehemiah's words brought the courage and hope the people needed, and his commitment and enthusiasm rubbed off on them. We all need to hear words of encouragement. Our encouraging words of testimony to God's gracious work can encourage fellow believers to work together to accomplish God's work.

When Judah's enemies learned of Nehemiah's plan to rebuild the wall, they tried to stop the project with mocking, ridicule, and threats. Sanballat, governor of Samaria, and Tobiah, governor of Ammon, had already made their displeasure known (Neh. 2:10). Geshem ruled a confederation of Arab tribes. Since his territory included Edom and the southern part of Judah, he also would have seen Nehemiah's appointment as governor of Judah a threat to his power. The three leaders ridiculed the Jews' plan to rebuild Jerusalem's wall and accused them of rebellion against Artaxerxes.

Nehemiah answered the governors calmly but forcefully. He first stated God's involvement in the project and noted He would bring success. Nehemiah then declared the governors had no authority in Judah and Jerusalem. Artaxerxes had appointed him governor. By the power of God and the permission of the king, the people would rebuild.

FOR FURTHER STUDY

What factors encouraged Nehemiah to take steps of faith? What factors help you take steps of faith?

3. Reporting Progress (Neh. 3:1-32)

Verse 1: **Eliashib the high priest and his fellow priests began rebuilding the Sheep Gate. They dedicated it and installed its doors. ⌊After building the wall⌋ to the Tower of the Hundred and the Tower of Hananel, they dedicated it.**

Everyone participated in the rebuilding, including Eliashib [ih LIGH uh shib], the high priest. Since the **Sheep Gate** stood near the temple area close to the northeast corner of the wall, the priests had great interest in its restoration. The Sheep Gate probably received its name because sheep passed through the gate on their way to being sacrificed. The priests continued their work **to the Tower of the Hundred and the Tower of Hananel** [HAN uh nehl]. Both towers lay along the northern section of the wall.

The use of the word **rebuilding** rather than repairing suggests the extensive destruction along the northern wall. When the Babylonians attacked Jerusalem in 587 B.C. the northern wall sustained the greatest damage.

Verse 2: **The men of Jericho built next to Eliashib, and next to them Zaccur son of Imri built.**

The rebuilding drew people from outside Jerusalem. God used Nehemiah to give the people a new vision and help them work cooperatively to make that vision a reality. Rebuilding the wall required organization and hard work. Nehemiah divided the wall into sections to accomplish the task. Sections varied in length and various individuals bore responsibility for each section. In some cases inhabitants rebuilt the wall close to their homes.

Nehemiah not only succeeded in organizing the rebuilding, he brought people together to work cooperatively on the project. First, he drew people from towns outside Jerusalem including Tekoa (3:5), Gibeon (3:7), Mizpah (3:7), and Zanoah (3:13). Second, Nehemiah brought in a variety of people who had limited experience in construction such as goldsmiths and perfumers (3:8). Third, district administrators participated (3:9,12). Finally, Nehemiah enlisted women in the construction (3:12). Nehemiah's ability to enlist people from diverse backgrounds as workers and lead them in a cooperative effort indicated God's empowering of Nehemiah.

Despite Nehemiah's best efforts, not everyone participated in the rebuilding. The nobles of Tekoa refused to help (3:5). No matter how hard we try we will encounter resistance and not everyone will work with us. Rather than be discouraged by a lack of participation on the part of a few, we need to work with those who volunteer and rejoice in their participation.

FOR FURTHER STUDY
How did Nehemiah encourage believers to work together? How can you encourage believers to work in your community to accomplish God's will?

The Week of January 7

DEVISING STRATEGIES

Background Passage: Nehemiah 4:1–7:73
Lesson Passages: Nehemiah 4:1-2,4,12-13,19-20,22; 6:2-3,11-13

INTRODUCTION

A church opens a mission center in a depressed urban area. Knowing the potential of the center to change lives, drug dealers encourage local youth to vandalize the building. When police identify some of the youth involved, the mission staff asks if the youth can repaint the facilities. Under the concerned prayers and ministry of the mission staff, three young men make decisions for Christ and turn their lives around.

Another church seeks to move to a new subdivision. When some residents discover the church's plan, they organize and ask the city council to rezone the area to prohibit church buildings. Church members pray, begin a public relations campaign, and hire an attorney to represent them before the city council. After discussion and compromise between the two groups, the church receives permission to locate in the subdivision.

Ministry for Christ sometimes leads to clashes with unbelievers who oppose the church in their attempts to avoid the call of Christ on their lives. Churches may face ridicule, hostility, intimidation, or legal action. Believers always need to pray, but believers also can develop and use other sound, ethical strategies to work through or around obstacles to ministry.

Trusting and obeying God in hostile circumstances involves prayer, courage, and strategy. Rather than imitating the world, we need to devise and employ strategies that seek to facilitate ministry and redeem those who oppose us. Nehemiah employed a variety of strategies to enable the Jews to rebuild Jerusalem's wall. His plans and work resulted in the wall's completion; a renewed spirit of cooperation, compassion, and obedience among the Jews; and the recognition by his enemies that God had acted for His people.

Nehemiah 4:1–7:73
1. Trowels and Swords (Neh. 4:1-23)
2. Injustice and Oppression (Neh. 5:1-19)
3. Deceit and Intimidation (Neh. 6:1-19)
4. Organization and Registration (Neh. 7:1-73)

THE BACKGROUND

As rebuilding of Jerusalem's wall began, Sanballat [san BAL uht], the governor of Samaria, ridiculed the Jews' efforts. Tobiah [toh BIGH uh], the governor of Ammon, joined Sanballat in discouraging the rebuilding. Nehemiah viewed their ridicule as directed against God and asked God to judge them for their sin. The Jews continued to work rebuilding the wall to half its height. As a result Sanballat, Tobiah, and others plotted to attack Jerusalem. Nehemiah stationed guards and gathered the people to encourage them. All the workers carried weapons with half working while the other half stood guard. Nehemiah also established a signal so that if enemies attacked, the workers could quickly run to the point of the attack and repel the enemies. All workers remained in Jerusalem during the rebuilding with Nehemiah and the men with him setting the example (Neh. 4:1-23).

While dealing with external threats, Nehemiah also faced internal problems. Those rebuilding the wall had no time to pursue their livelihoods, yet they still had to feed their families. Wealthier Jews who loaned money at interest to the workers took advantage of their plight. Nehemiah confronted the guilty nobles and officials, and they agreed to cancel the interest and collateral. Nehemiah had earlier set an example by refusing his special privileges as governor (5:1-19).

When the Jews had completed the wall with the exception of installing the gates, their enemies tried to lure Nehemiah out of Jerusalem. When he refused, they accused the Jews of rebellion against Persia. Nehemiah discounted the rumors, and the enemies then used the false prophet Shemaiah [shih MAY yuh] to encourage Nehemiah to hide in the temple from his enemies. Knowing such behavior would break God's law and set a bad example, Nehemiah refused. He asked God to judge his enemies for their sins. Within 52 days the Jews completed the wall despite the opposition of their enemies (6:1-19).

Jerusalem still had few inhabitants. Nehemiah organized the city and then found an old list that registered them according to their genealogy. He used the list to repopulate Jerusalem and make the city more defensible (Neh. 7:1-73).

THE BIBLE PASSAGE

1. Trowels and Swords (Neh. 4:1-23)

Verse 1: **When Sanballat heard that we were rebuilding the wall, he became furious. He mocked the Jews**

Sanballat, the governor of Samaria, had greeted Nehemiah's arrival in Jerusalem with displeasure (2:10). Upon hearing that rebuilding of

Jerusalem's wall had begun, he **became furious**. The successful rebuilding of the wall would add to Nehemiah's prestige and authority as governor of Judah and weaken Sanballat's power and status. Unable to complain to Artaxerxes since he had approved the project and commissioned Nehemiah as governor, Sanballat employed ridicule in an attempt to halt the project. Using psychological warfare, he hoped to discourage the Jews and boost his own and his people's morale.

Verse 2: **before his colleagues and the powerful men of Samaria, and said, "What are these pathetic Jews doing? Can they restore ⌊it⌋ by themselves? Will they offer sacrifices? Will they ever finish it? Can they bring these burnt stones back to life from the mounds of rubble?"**

Sanballat began his campaign of ridicule during a speech to **his colleagues and the powerful men of Samaria**. The Hebrew word translated *powerful men* also can be translated "army." As a governor, Sanballat commanded a contingent of Persian soldiers or local militia that could provide security for Samaria and aid Artaxerxes in his battles. Perhaps he assembled his troops for a military show of force or perhaps he simply addressed the officials and powerful men who surrounded him in Samaria. His audience consisted of individuals who agreed with him and thus constituted the ideal group to hear and applaud his taunts of the Jews.

Sanballat asked five questions designed to belittle the Jews and their rebuilding efforts. Sanballat's first, second, and fourth questions emphasized the small number and weakness of the Jews. Judah constituted a small province. Jerusalem lay in ruins without a wall and with few inhabitants. Sanballat and his officials laughed at the idea of such a small group accomplishing such a great task.

Sanballat's third question ridiculed the Jews and God. The **sacrifices** might refer to offerings to God either at the laying of the foundation or at the completion of the rebuilding. The Jews may have offered an initial offering to God when they laid the wall's foundation, but Sanballat stated their inability to complete the wall would cancel any plan of offering sacrifices at the wall's completion.

Coupling the third question with the fifth question provides another understanding. Sanballat may have mocked God. The Samaritan governor may have falsely thought the Lord lacked power to help His people rebuild the wall. Would God respond to the people's sacrifices by animating the stones so they would rise from the ruins and take their place in the wall? Sanballat described the stones as **burnt**. Limestone, like that used in biblical Jerusalem, weakens and crumbles after being burned. Probably Sanballat exaggerated the condition of the building materials to further mock the Jews' efforts. Sanballat ridiculed the Jews' faith and God. From their enemies' viewpoint, the Jews faced too many obstacles to complete the project.

Tobiah, the governor of Ammon, shared Sanballat's displeasure regarding events in Judah (Neh. 2:10,19) and joined him in mocking the Jews. Ancient armies used siege weapons to break down walls and gain entry into cities. The process required time and effort. Tobiah suggested the weight of a fox leaping on Jerusalem's wall would cause the wall to crumble (4:3). Tobiah's words were not true at all because excavated remnants of Nehemiah's wall have shown it was about nine feet thick.

Verse 4: **Listen, our God, for we are despised. Make their insults return on their own heads and let them be taken as plunder to a land of captivity.**

Nehemiah's response to Sanballat's and Tobiah's comments seems harsh to Christian ears, but Old Testament writers often asked God to judge their enemies (for example, Ps. 79:6-7; Jer. 18:19-23). Since God had sent Nehemiah to lead the Jews in rebuilding the wall, he believed that although Sanballat and Tobiah aimed their ridicule at the people, they really ridiculed God. Nehemiah asked God to judge the individuals who insulted Him.

Nehemiah's prayer encompassed four ideas. First, Nehemiah wanted God to judge his enemies' sin by allowing them to reap what they had sown (Neh. 4:5). The people of Judah had rebelled against God, and God had punished them with exile. Nehemiah suggested God not forgive the enemies' sins until they received the same punishment. Second, Nehemiah asked God to act to judge the Jews' enemies. Nehemiah did not form a terrorist force to assassinate his enemies or strike their families. He trusted God to avenge His name and people. Third, Nehemiah's prayer revealed his zeal for serving and glorifying God. Fourth, Nehemiah's words served to encourage the people. Nehemiah encouraged them to trust in God who would help them accomplish the rebuilding and punish their enemies for their sins.

Despite the ridicule, the Jews continued rebuilding and soon had the wall completed to half its height. Success generated greater anger among their enemies. Sanballat assembled an alliance against Judah that surrounded the small province on all four sides. The allies plotted to attack Jerusalem in hopes the Jews would abandon the project (4:6-8).

Nehemiah and the Jews prayed and acted. Nehemiah stationed guards around the city day and night to watch for possible attack. The people continued the rebuilding but with less enthusiasm. Their enemies' psychological warfare through ridicule and military threat created additional discouragement (4:9-11). Without quick action, the project might come to a halt.

FOR FURTHER STUDY
Nehemiah's strategy for handling mockery was to recognize its source and to pray. How can confidence in God help us withstand mockery?

Verse 12: **When the Jews who lived nearby arrived, they said to us time and again, "Everywhere you turn, ⌊they⌋ attack us."**

Judah's enemies had spread rumors of an impending attack on Jerusalem. The **Jews who lived nearby** came to Jerusalem and pleaded with their family and friends to abandon the rebuilding. Those who lived outside Jerusalem may have had two concerns. First, they did not want their loved ones to die in an attack on Jerusalem. Second, they may have believed if the people halted the rebuilding, the enemies would leave Judah alone. The pleas of loved ones certainly tempted the workers to leave Jerusalem.

Verse 13: **So I stationed ⌊people⌋ behind the lowest sections of the wall, at the vulnerable areas. I stationed them by families with their swords, spears, and bows.**

Nehemiah's action accomplished two objectives. First, the presence of armed men at the weaker sections would discourage the enemy from attacking a vulnerable part of the wall. Second, Nehemiah probably gathered not only a guard at the weaker sections but also more people. Sanballat and his allies probably had spies watching to see if construction would cease. Instead of seeing a mass desertion from Jerusalem, they saw a gathering of all the people and preparations to repel any attack.

Nehemiah arranged the people **by families.** Grouping the people by families gave them an opportunity to see the loved ones for whom they built and fought and thereby strengthened their motivation. Nehemiah called the people back to their obligation to protect their families and land.

At Nehemiah's request, the men assembled armed for battle. Swords were used in hand-to-hand combat. Bows served as long-range weapons. Spies watching the assembly could report to Sanballat that rather than abandoning their work, the Jews were prepared to meet any military challenge.

As the people stood holding their weapons, Nehemiah reminded them of their real strength—God. The Jews needed to remember God's past salvation and believe God would act again to deliver them. Yet they also needed to prepare to fight. Nehemiah called for both faith and action (4:14).

When Sanballat and his allies learned of the Jews' preparation, they abandoned their plan. Nehemiah gave God the glory for discouraging the enemies and uniting the Jews (4:15), but he continued to organize Jerusalem's defense. While half of the men worked, the other half stood guard in full battle gear. Even those who worked carried weapons with them (4:16-18).

FOR FURTHER STUDY

Nehemiah effectively organized the people to withstand opposition, and he encouraged them. How can organization and encouragement help a church function smoothly despite opposition to accomplish God's purpose?

Verse 19: **Then I said to the nobles, the officials, and the rest of the people: "The work is enormous and spread out, and we are separated far from one another along the wall.**

Despite Nehemiah's plans for rebuilding and guarding against attack, his work crews spread out along the wall left any section vulnerable to attack. Having solved one problem, Nehemiah did not rest on past successes. He constantly thought and planned for Jerusalem's defense and the people's security.

Verse 20: **Wherever you hear the trumpet sound, rally to us there. Our God will fight for us!"**

Nehemiah continued to supervise the rebuilding, watch for enemies, and rethink his strategy. He instructed the people that in the event of an attack, a trumpeter would sound a blast calling everyone to that section of the wall to defend the city.

Nehemiah again reminded the people God served as their greatest strength and would fight to deliver them. He had delivered His people from Egypt (Ex. 14:14), brought them into Canaan (Josh. 23:10), and, if they obeyed, would help them defeat any enemy (Deut. 20:4). God's help did not mean the people only had to sit back and watch God fight. God's help meant they could join with Him in the confidence that His presence and power would be with them. The people worked from dawn to dusk rebuilding the wall (Neh. 4:21). They accompanied their trust in God with dedication and diligence.

Verse 22: **At that time, I also said to the people, "Let everyone and his servant spend the night inside Jerusalem, so that they can stand guard by night and work by day."**

Nehemiah dealt with another dangerous situation. Many of the Jews who lived in neighboring towns walked to their homes at night and then to Jerusalem the next morning. The practice posed several dangers. First, enemies could easily attack the workers. Second, enemies could quietly join groups of workers and sneak into Jerusalem to cause trouble. Third, workers who became discouraged by the difficult work and continued threat could go home and not return. Nehemiah insisted all workers remain in Jerusalem until the wall stood strong again. The presence of all the workers inside the city also allowed Nehemiah to post more guards in shifts around the walls at night.

All leaders can model themselves after Nehemiah. He possessed great faith in God and commitment to His work, but also he thought and worked diligently to organize the rebuilding and protect the people. Nehemiah also set a positive example by following the directives he gave to others (4:23). Most believers do not face physical attack from those who oppose them, although some believers do. As we serve God, we all need to look to Him for courage, strength, and guidance; prepare strategies to meet difficulties we may face with compassion and determination; and work side-by-side with others.

FOR FURTHER STUDY
    List traits that made Nehemiah a good leader. How can you become a more effective leader?

2. Injustice and Oppression (Neh. 5:1-19)

While enemies threatened Judah from outside, poverty threatened the people from inside. The Jews brought three complaints to Nehemiah (5:1-5). First, those with large families needed food but had no time to pursue their profession and either grow food or earn money to buy food. They requested food to keep their families alive. Second, the need to purchase food had forced those who owned land to mortgage it, thus adding to their financial burden. Third, some Jews had borrowed money to pay the heavy taxes demanded by the Persian Empire. Interest charged by the wealthier Jews who loaned money could reach 40 percent. Some had no choice but to place their children into debt slavery and allow them to work for the creditor until the debt had been paid.

The social injustice enraged Nehemiah and drove him to action (5:6-13). He accused the wealthy Jews of taking advantage of those less fortunate. He called an assembly of the people to address the problem. Nehemiah reprimanded them for disobeying God by charging interest to their own people (see Deut. 23:19) and called them to obey God's command.

Recognizing their guilt, the Jewish creditors agreed to do as Nehemiah requested (Neh. 5:12-13). Nehemiah summoned the priests and had the creditors join him in a sacred oath to do what they had promised. Many Jews carried personal belongings in the folds of their robes. Nehemiah shook the folds of his robes letting objects he carried fall to the ground. This action symbolized that all who failed to keep their promise would be shaken by God until they possessed nothing. In response the people took the oath, praised God, and then acted on their promise.

Nehemiah practiced what he preached (5:14-19). During his term as governor from 445 to 433 B.C., he refused to exercise his right to collect taxes for his own needs even though previous governors and their officials had used and abused taxation to live in luxury. Nehemiah also refused to purchase land. Instead of abusing his authority and enriching himself, he devoted all his energy to rebuilding the wall and helping his people. Nehemiah placed the people's needs before his own, thereby proving himself to be a great leader and man of God.

3. Deceit and Intimidation (Neh. 6:1-19)

Having dealt with the internal problems, Nehemiah faced yet another external problem. Under his supervision the men of Judah had completed the wall but had not yet installed the gates. When Sanballat, Tobiah, and Geshem [GESH ehm] learned of the wall's completion, they plotted against Nehemiah once more (6:1).

Verse 2: Sanballat and Geshem sent me a message: "Come, let's meet together in the villages of the Ono Valley." But they were planning to harm me.

While Geshem had been involved in the earlier alliance against Nehemiah (2:19), he played a more active role with Sanballat in their new plot. Sanballat and Geshem invited Nehemiah to one of **the villages of the Ono Valley.** This area lay distant from Jerusalem's defenses and closer to Sanballat and his troops. Clearly Sanballat and Geshem intended to lure Nehemiah from Jerusalem and kill him. From his earlier dealings with them, Nehemiah realized their true intentions.

Verse 3: So I sent messengers to them, saying, "I am doing a great work and cannot come down. Why should the work cease while I leave it and go down to you?"

Nehemiah politely refused their invitation. He even added a touch of humor by referring to his involvement in the rebuilding of the wall as his excuse for not coming. He knew full well that halting the rebuilding served as the sole purpose of the invitation. Nehemiah refused to be distracted from his God-given work. He remained steadfast in his commitment.

Nehemiah's refusal did not deter Sanballat (6:4-7). "Four times" (6:4) Sanballat invited Nehemiah to meet with him. Perhaps he hoped to wear Nehemiah down until he agreed. When Nehemiah still refused, Sanballat asked a fifth time. This time he sent an aide with an unsealed letter so anyone could read it. In the letter Sanballat and Geshem accused Nehemiah of rebuilding Jerusalem's wall in preparation to rebel against King Artaxerxes. They suggested Nehemiah planned to become king and had already enlisted prophets to proclaim his legitimacy.

Nehemiah declared the rumors of rebellion to be groundless and false (6:8-9). He had faithfully served Artaxerxes as his cupbearer and continued to serve him as a governor. He refused to negotiate with individuals who lied. Instead he placed his trust in God.

After Nehemiah's response to Sanballat's and Geshem's charges, he visited the prophet Shemaiah (6:10). Shemaiah warned Nehemiah to flee to the temple for protection because enemies planned on killing him that very night. Not everyone in Judah favored or participated in the rebuilding (3:5) and some individuals may have found Nehemiah's strict measures for rebuilding the wall and maintaining social order intolerable. Shemaiah's words could have discouraged a lesser leader than Nehemiah.

Verse 11: **But I said, "Should a man like me run away? How can I enter the temple and live? I will not go."**

Nehemiah's questions indicated he believed Shemaiah did not speak for God. Nehemiah doubted that God expected one whom He appointed as a leader to run away when danger threatened. A true prophet would not encourage a person to abandon God's call. Therefore Nehemiah ignored Shemaiah's warning.

FOR FURTHER STUDY

How do you determine whether someone is truly speaking on behalf of God?

Verse 12: **I realized that God had not sent him, because of the prophecy he spoke against me. Tobiah and Sanballat had hired him.**

Nehemiah realized Shemaiah's words constituted yet another plan on the part of Tobiah and Sanballat to remove him and leave his work unfinished.

Verse 13: **He was hired, so that I would be intimidated, do as he suggested, sin, and get a bad reputation, in order that they could discredit me.**

If Nehemiah had followed Shemaiah's prophecy and hidden in the temple for protection, the people would have questioned Nehemiah's leadership abilities and his commitment as their leader. Following Shemaiah's advice would have given Nehemiah a **bad reputation** and discredited him, thus destroying his influence with the people.

Nehemiah realized not everyone who claims to speak for God truly speaks for Him. People can use holy language for their own purposes rather than for speaking God's Word to challenge and comfort a world in need. We need to evaluate the words we hear to determine their consistency with God's Word, His love, and His desire to save. Nehemiah's trust in God and his personal integrity gave him the insight to recognize God's truth and the courage to maintain his convictions even under threat. By holding firmly to God's revealed truth and our integrity, we also can cope with and triumph over manipulation.

Again Nehemiah turned to God in prayer and asked that He remember and judge Tobiah and Sanballat for working against Him (Neh. 6:14). Nehemiah also mentioned others who had hoped to intimidate him. Nehemiah had enemies inside and outside Jerusalem but rather than attack them, he trusted God to deal with them in His time.

Under Nehemiah's direction and encouragement, the men of Judah rebuilt Jerusalem's wall in only 52 days (6:15). They completed the project near the end of the month Elul [IH luhl] (early October). Amazingly the events of Nehemiah 2:1–6:19 occurred over a period of six months. For Nehemiah to have received permission from Artaxerxes to rebuild the wall, prepared and made the journey, rallied the people, dealt with external and internal threats, and completed the wall within six months testifies to God's work through the great leader Nehemiah.

The swift completion of the wall despite opposition amazed Judah's neighbors. The nations that had attempted to intimidate Judah found themselves intimidated by the incredible power of God. In the face of God's work among His people, the nations lost the will to oppose the Jews and finally recognized the reality and power of God (6:16).

The account of rebuilding the wall concluded with information regarding Tobiah (6:17-19). Though he served Persia as governor of Ammon, he had influential friends in Jerusalem. Tobiah's friends opposed Nehemiah as well and helped Tobiah intimidate Nehemiah by keeping Tobiah informed regarding events in Jerusalem while simultaneously singing his praises to Nehemiah. Despite Tobiah's underhanded methods, Nehemiah accomplished God's will through faith in God and skillful leadership.

4. Organization and Registration (Neh. 7:1-73)

Completion of the wall did not mean Nehemiah had finished his work. He still needed to organize the city (7:1-3). The gatekeepers normally guarded the temple's entrance, but because of the dangers Jerusalem faced, Nehemiah assigned them to the city gates. Both the singers and Levites had always worked closely with the gatekeepers, so Nehemiah assigned them to aid the gatekeepers. Nehemiah appointed two faithful individuals—his brother Hanani, along with Hananiah—to govern Jerusalem. Nehemiah then created a schedule for opening the gates and for guard duty.

Noticing the small population in Jerusalem, Nehemiah realized he needed to increase the population to protect the city and provide for its long-term growth (7:4-5). He knew he needed to move some of the people who lived in the outlying villages into Jerusalem, but he did not want to uproot every family of some groups while leaving other groups untouched.

Before he could begin his own census he found the list of families who had returned from exile (7:6-73). Instead of taking a new census, Nehemiah used the list to draw people from each group to repopulate Jerusalem.

FOR FURTHER STUDY
Read the article entitled "Walls" on pages 1658-1659 of the *Holman Illustrated Bible Dictionary*. Note especially the symbolism of walls. List three reasons rebuilding Jerusalem's wall would have been important for physical protection and spiritual growth.

The Week of January 14
REDEDICATING LIVES

Background Passage: Nehemiah 8:1–10:39
Lesson Passages: Nehemiah 8:1,5-6,9-10; 9:1-2,38; 10:28-29

INTRODUCTION

As Frank left the revival service, he said to his friend Ben, "I can tell you even before a revival begins who is going to rededicate their lives to Christ. It is the same people every time. Angela always comes crying up the aisle. Trent always comes down and wants to address the congregation about how he plans to change his life. We could have been out a lot sooner!"

"Don't be too hard on them," Ben responded. "True, the same people often come forward, but I'm not sure we should dismiss them as insincere. Angela has a hard life working and raising those teenagers by herself. I appreciate her desire to be a godly parent. And Trent has made some significant changes in his life and business in the last ten years. I think he realizes how he still needs to change and genuinely wants God to help him make those changes."

"Well, yes, but it just seems you can rededicate your life too often. Isn't walking to the front of the church once, enough?"

"Whether we rededicate our lives to Christ publicly or privately, we all need to regularly evaluate our lives, confess our sins, and follow God with renewed dedication. I did not publicly rededicate my life tonight, but as I stood singing the final hymn, I asked God to forgive me and help me live in a way more pleasing to Him. Trent and I are having coffee tomorrow morning to pray together. Would you like to join us?"

Accepting Christ as Savior is the beginning point. As we follow Him, we all fall prey to temptations. Our actions and attitudes disappoint God and make us insensitive to His guidance. We all need to evaluate our lives, confess our sins, and return to God with a renewed desire and commitment to serve Him.

Nehemiah 8:1–10:39
1. Conviction of God's Word (Neh. 8:1-18)
2. Confession of Sins (Neh. 9:1-37)
3. Commitment to the Covenant (Neh. 9:38–10:39)

THE BACKGROUND

In the seventh month the Israelites asked Ezra to bring God's law to a special assembly. For six hours Ezra read the law and the Levites interpreted the law so the people could understand God's directions for living. As the people realized their sins, they wept. Nehemiah, Ezra, and the Levites encouraged the people not to weep but to celebrate because the day was a festival to praise God and rejoice. The next day the people began preparations for the Festival of Tabernacles or Booths. During the festival, Ezra read from God's law and taught the people God's commands (Neh. 8:1-18).

On the 24th day of the 7th month the Israelites gathered again while wearing sackcloth and placing dust on their heads. The people confessed their sins and those of their ancestors. They remembered God's gracious acts to Israel and the people's continued rebellion against God. They praised God as Creator and Redeemer and confessed the Israelites' sins in the wilderness as Moses led them to Canaan. Despite the people's rebellion, God brought His people into Canaan. When another generation rebelled, God allowed Israel's enemies to overcome them but when the Israelites cried out, God again delivered His people. The people acknowledged their present situation resulted from their sins and asked God to intervene to restore them. To symbolize Israel's commitment to God, the leaders wrote out a binding agreement in which they pledged to obey God (9:1-37).

Priests, Levites, and other leaders signed the agreement and the rest of the people verbally bound themselves to obey God's law. The people promised not to allow their children to marry outside their faith community. The Israelites also promised not to conduct business on the Sabbath and to celebrate the Sabbath Year. They promised to faithfully pay the annual temple tax and to offer God their tithes and offerings to support the temple and its personnel (9:38–10:39).

THE BIBLE PASSAGE

1. Conviction of God's Word (Neh. 8:1-18)

Verse 1: **all the people gathered together at the square in front of the Water Gate. They asked Ezra the scribe to bring the book of the law of Moses that the LORD had given Israel.**

Bible students hold differing opinions regarding how the events of Nehemiah 8–10 fit into the chronology of Ezra's and Nehemiah's work in Jerusalem. Some Bible students place the assembly shortly after Ezra's arrival in Jerusalem (Ezra 7:8-9; 8:31-32). Having been given authority by Artaxerxes to use God's law for administering Judah (7:26), Ezra read and interpreted the law publicly at a special assembly two months after his arrival.

Other Bible students think the assembly occurred 13 years after Ezra's arrival in Jerusalem and followed his dealing with the problem of foreign wives (Ezra 10:1-17). Probably Ezra had assembled the people several times during the 13-year period to teach them the law. The people's desire to have Ezra read the law indicated they already felt convicted by their failure to keep God's law and desired to publicly rededicate their lives to God. No matter when the assembly occurred, the people's desire for Ezra to read extensively from the law seems to indicate Ezra had been teaching them for some time.

The seventh month comprised an important month in the Jewish calendar. The Festival of Trumpets began on the first day of the seventh month, the exact day the Israelites assembled to have Ezra read the law. The Day of Atonement occurred on the 10th day of the 7th month (Lev. 23:27) and the Festival of Tabernacles or Booths began on the 15th day (Lev. 23:34). During the Festival of Booths in a Sabbath Year all Israelites were to assemble and the priests were to read the law (Deut. 31:10-11). The seventh month provided an appropriate time for a national rededication service.

FOR FURTHER STUDY

Read the article entitled "Festivals" on pages 567-573 of the *Holman Illustrated Bible Dictionary*. How do religious celebrations help strengthen our faith in God?

The people of Judah, who represented all Israel after the destruction of the Northern Kingdom, assembled not at the temple but **at the square in front of the Water Gate**. The Water Gate lay on the southeast side of the city. If the assembly had occurred in the temple, only the men could have entered the inner court and heard Ezra's reading of the law. The people assembled outside the temple so men, women, and children could hear the law read and interpreted (Neh. 8:2). The location for the reading also suggests the people needed to understand that faithful obedience to God's law in daily life was far more important than mere attendance at temple services and offering sacrifices.

The people asked Ezra to bring **the book of the law of Moses** to the assembly. The book probably included the first five books of the Bible known as the Torah or Pentateuch. Ezra may have brought the scrolls for all five books but probably read from selected sections since he only read for approximately six hours (8:3).

Significantly, the people took the lead in the rededication service. Ezra's teaching and God's Spirit at work had convinced them they needed to turn to God in faithful obedience. Spiritual renewal occurs when God's people seek Him.

Ezra responded to the people's request and brought the law to the assembled crowd. The assembly included men, women, and the children who were old enough to understand and respond to God's claim on their lives. The people had planned for this special assembly. The community had constructed a platform on which Ezra could stand so the people could more easily see and hear him. Thirteen lay leaders also had been selected to stand on the platform with him. Their presence indicated the secular leadership joined with the religious leadership in obeying God's law. Ezra read from the law from daybreak until noon, a period of about six hours, and the people listened attentively (8:2-4). Their attentiveness emphasized their deep desire to understand God's standards.

Most of us find it difficult to imagine standing and listening to someone read the Bible for nearly six hours. Perhaps if we did not have such easy access to the Bible through printed Bibles, electronic Bibles, Bible study books, and commentaries, we would hunger for hearing God's Word the way the assembled Israelites did. As believers who claim the Bible as our book of faith and guidance, we need to treasure and respect God's Word. Reading long passages from the Bible helps us broaden and deepen our understanding of God and His will.

FOR FURTHER STUDY

In what ways do you think believers can be encouraged to read and study more of the Bible?

Verse 5: Ezra opened the book in full view of all the people, since he was elevated above everyone. As he opened it, all the people stood up.

Scripture became available in book form considerably after Ezra's time, so Ezra read from a scroll. As Ezra unrolled the scroll, the people stood, thereby indicating their reverence and respect for God's law. They realized the words Ezra would read came from God Himself, who deserved their praise, adoration, and obedience. The people remained standing throughout Ezra's reading of the law.

Verse 6: Ezra blessed the LORD, the great God, and with their hands uplifted all the people said, " Amen, Amen!" Then they bowed down and worshiped the LORD with their faces to the ground.

Before reading the law, Ezra **blessed the LORD**. In Israel a blessing typically preceded the reading of Scripture. The idea of blessing God may seem strange. On the one hand, God certainly does not need our blessings. As Creator and Ruler of the universe, no one can frustrate His purposes. God's purpose will be accomplished, and He will one day be recognized by all as Lord of all (Phil. 2:10-11). On the other hand, blessing God comprises an important act of worship. When we bless God, we acknowledge Him as the source of life and thank Him for the many blessings He has given us. The Bible comprises one of God's greatest gifts to us. Blessing God before reading from His Word is an appropriate act of worship.

Ezra referred to God as **the great God**. Many people in the ancient Near East, including the Persians, referred to certain gods as great. Ezra attributed greatness to God alone because only God exists and rules. People of other religions might claim their gods were great, but those gods did not exist. Only God deserves the title *great*.

The people responded in three ways. First, they lifted their hands. Typically people in the ancient Near East lifted their hands when they prayed. The lifting of hands symbolized the worshipers' dependence on God to supply their needs (Ezra 9:5; Ps. 28:2). Second, the people spoke a double **Amen**. The word *Amen* derives from a Hebrew verb meaning "to confirm." By saying *Amen* the people confirmed their faith in God and acknowledged their responsibility to obey His guidance. Third, the people **bowed down and worshiped**. People bowed down to those who had authority over them, such as kings. When the people bowed down before God, they indicated their submission to Him. The people's response indicated their recognition of God as Lord of life and their willingness to live by His standards.

The Israelites valued their opportunity to hear God's law. Before they had heard one word read, they responded with reverence toward God and His guidance. We also need to approach the Bible with reverence and awe, treasuring God's words and committing to obey Him.

Under the dominance of the Assyrian, Babylonian, and Persian Empires, most Jews in Judah and Babylon learned the international diplomatic language, Aramaic. Through successive generations the Jews primarily spoke Aramaic and used Hebrew typically for religious rites. Although Aramaic and Hebrew were kindred languages, most of the Jews listening to Ezra would have understood Aramaic far better than Hebrew. Thus, as Ezra read sections, 13 Levites explained the law to the people, probably standing among the crowd and translating the Hebrew passages into Aramaic so the people near them could understand (Neh. 8:7-8).

The Israelites did not want to simply hear words read. They wanted to understand the words, so they could apply them in daily life. We also need to understand and apply God's Word today. When we listen to the Bible read in a worship service or read the Bible in a study group or in private devotional time, we need to concentrate so we can understand God's direction and discover how to apply God's guidance in daily life.

Verse 9: Nehemiah the governor, Ezra the priest and scribe, and the Levites who were instructing the people said to all of them, "This day is holy to the LORD your God. Do not mourn or weep." For all the people were weeping as they heard the words of the law.

For the first time, the Bible mentions Nehemiah and Ezra working together. Ezra arrived in Jerusalem before Nehemiah. Following Nehemiah's completion of Jerusalem's wall, the two worked together in leading the people in understanding God's law and rededicating themselves to God.

The reading and interpretation of God's law drew an appropriate response from the people. Realizing their disobedience to God, they wept. While the people reacted appropriately to being convicted of their sins, the Festival of Trumpets was supposed to be a time of rejoicing rather than weeping. Nehemiah, Ezra, and the Levites urged the people not to weep, explaining the day was **holy to the LORD**. God had decreed the first day of the seventh month be a day of joy (Lev. 23:23-25).

The Israelites had two reasons to rejoice. First, they had realized their sins and repented. Second, they could celebrate God's grace and forgiveness that had freed them from their sins just as God had earlier freed Israel from Egyptian slavery and brought the people home from Babylonian captivity. Rather than wallowing in their sins and unworthiness, the people needed to rejoice in God's mercy and in the new life they could find in Him.

Verse 10: **Then he said to them, "Go and eat what is rich, drink what is sweet, and send portions to those who have nothing prepared, since today is holy to our Lord. Do not grieve, because your strength ⌐comes from⌐ rejoicing in the LORD."**

The Israelites needed to worship as the occasion demanded. They needed to feast on the richest meats and drink the sweetest drinks, rejoicing in God's provisions of life and salvation. The people also needed to provide for those without rich meats and sweet drinks, so they could enjoy the celebration as well. Most likely, they could not afford the food and drink for the feast.

God intended the celebration to remind the Israelites their strength came from **rejoicing in the LORD**. The Israelites could have continued to mourn because of their sins, but God wanted them to recognize and rejoice in His goodness and love. Rejoicing in God enabled the Israelites to live obediently and find strength for and joy in each day.

The Levites successfully calmed the people and impressed on them the need to celebrate. The people prepared the feast and began to celebrate God's provision of salvation and the necessities of physical life. Those who had shared with those who did not, so all could fully participate in the feast. Through sharing with others, the people realized God's goodness and trusted Him to provide for them in the coming year (Neh. 8:11-12).

The next day a smaller group composed of family leaders, priests, and Levites assembled for a Bible study led by Ezra. As they studied God's law, they discovered God had decreed the Festival of Booths be celebrated beginning on the 15th day of the 7th month. The festival not only celebrated God's provision of the harvest but also commemorated Israel's living in temporary shelters in the wilderness after God brought the Israelites out of Egypt. To celebrate the festival properly the Israelites needed to dwell in booths during the festival (Lev. 23:33-43), so the people needed to gather branches immediately to build the temporary shelters. The leaders quickly spread the word throughout Judah and instructed the people how to prepare for the festival. The people responded with joy. They built booths on their rooftops and courtyards and in the courts and squares of Jerusalem and lived in the booths for the entire festival. Not since the time of Joshua had the Israelites celebrated the Festival of Booths with such enthusiasm and joy. Each day during the festival, Ezra continued to read from God's law. On the final day, the people again assembled as God had directed (Neh. 8:13-18).

God's Word provides the guide for life. If we want to honor God with our lives and serve Him, we need to spend time reading and studying the whole Bible. Ignoring God's guidelines can cause us to drift from His purposes and ways. Focusing only on a small portion can deprive us of the blessings God has for us. Carefully listening to all God's Word helps us to remain focused and to mature as believers.

2. Confession of Sins (Neh. 9:1-37)

Verse 1: **On the twenty-fourth day of this month the Israelites assembled; they were fasting, ⌊wearing⌋ sackcloth, ⌊and had put⌋ dust on their heads.**

Having celebrated God's goodness, the Israelites gathered again for the solemn assembly that concluded the Festival of Booths (Lev. 23:33-36) to confess their sins. The Israelites expressed their grief over their sins and their desire to repent in three ways. First, the people fasted. The object of fasting or going without food was to focus on God and know God at a deeper level. The people's fasting indicated they desired to develop a closer fellowship with God. Second, the people wore **sackcloth,** a garment made from goat or camel hair. The wearing of sackcloth often accompanied mourning and repentance (Jonah 3:5,8) and seeking God (Dan. 9:3). The wearing of the uncomfortable clothing symbolized the people's humility and sorrow. Third, the people **put dust on their heads,** also a sign of mourning or of desperately seeking God. The three actions visibly symbolized the Israelites' inner grief, their plea for mercy, and their desire to know God.

Verse 2: **Those of Israelite descent separated themselves from all foreigners, and they stood and confessed their sins and the guilt of their fathers.**

The Israelites realized they needed to acknowledge their rebellion against God. They confessed both their sins and the sins of their ancestors. The people acknowledged they stood in a long line of sinners. Previous generations had disobeyed God even after He had delivered them from slavery in Egypt and brought them into Canaan. The sins of earlier generations had led to the Assyrian defeat of the Northern Kingdom of Israel and the Babylonian defeat of the Southern Kingdom of Judah. Rather than blame previous generations, the present generation identified with them. God's steadfast love had been constantly met with steadfast disobedience and the present generation understood themselves to be guilty as well.

For a fourth of the day the Israelites read from God's law and for another fourth they confessed their sins and worshiped. Levites led in the worship and confession (Neh. 9:3-5a).

The community's confession combined elements of psalms of confession (Ps. 106) and psalms recounting God's redeeming activity in Israel's history (Pss. 105; 135). Israel's confession began with blessing and general praise to God (Neh. 9:5b) and then specifically praised God as Creator (9:6). God's creation of all demonstrated His sovereignty over all. Confession begins with our recognition that the God against whom we have sinned is the Sovereign Lord who deserves our praise and obedience.

The Israelites recited God's grace and salvation throughout their history beginning with God's call and promises to Abraham (9:7-8). God had chosen Abraham, brought him to a new land, and promised him that land for his descendants. Abraham had responded in faith, thereby setting a model for all Israelites. Unfortunately, Israel did not follow Abraham's example, but God remained faithful to His promise.

Later in Israel's history God defeated the Egyptians, led Israel through the wilderness, provided His law to guide their lives, and met their physical needs (9:9-15). Yet, Israel responded not with thankful obedience but with stubborn disobedience. Even then God refused to abandon or destroy His people but continued to provide for and guide them (9:16-21).

God brought the Israelites into Canaan and used His people to punish the Canaanites for their immoral ways. God fulfilled His promise to Abraham to give him numerous descendants and a fruitful land. In response Israel disobeyed God again, so God allowed Israel's enemies to oppress His people. Yet when the people of Israel cried out for help, He raised up judges to deliver them. Generation after generation of Israelites rebelled, yet God continued to deliver His people until finally He punished them for their sins and rebellion by allowing them to be taken into captivity. Even then His love refused to give up on them (9:22-31).

The Israelites ended their prayer of confession by asking God to intervene in their current situation. They acknowledged the sins of their ancestors and themselves. They acknowledged God had consistently acted faithfully while they had continually disobeyed Him. Yet they asked God to see their plight as slaves and act to restore them (9:32-37).

When Scripture revealed the Israelites' sins, they confessed their sins, repented, and received God's forgiveness. When confronted by our sins, we need to do the same. We cannot pay for our own sins nor can we ever accumulate enough good deeds to offset our disobedience. God has paid for our sins through the death of His Son Jesus Christ. By confessing our sins, repenting, and turning to God through Christ, we can have a new, abundant life.

FOR FURTHER STUDY
What do you think is the value of confessing our sins?

3. Commitment to the Covenant (Neh. 9:38–10:39)

Chapter 9. Verse 38: **In view of all this, we are making a binding agreement in writing on a sealed document ⌊containing the names of⌋ our leaders, Levites, and priests.**

The Israelites who stood and confessed their sins genuinely intended to repent and follow God. They demonstrated their commitment by **making a binding agreement in writing**. The word *making* translates the Hebrew word "cut," a technical term for making a covenant that referred to the sacrificing of animals as part of the covenant ceremony. The word *agreement* does not translate the typical word for "covenant." The word shares the same root as the word "faithful" used to describe Abraham (9:8). As Abraham had been faithful to God, so the Israelites pledged to be faithful to Him.

The Israelite leaders, Levites, and priests signed their names to the agreement, thereby demonstrating their commitment to keeping the agreement and to serving as examples of faithfulness. Sealing the document ensured no one could tamper with it. The sealed agreement served as a reminder to the people of their decision to repent of their disobedience and live faithfully for God.

Nehemiah signed first, thus indicating his support as the most powerful local government leader (Neh. 10:1). Ezra apparently did not sign the document. Perhaps the Israelites saw Ezra as the mediator of the agreement rather than as a participant in the agreement. Alternatively, Ezra might have been represented in one of the priestly families whose leader signed the document. Those who signed the binding agreement represented all the government personnel, religious personnel, and families of the Israelites (10:2-27). All Israel committed to obeying God.

Chapter 10. Verse 28: **The rest of the people—the priests, Levites,** singers, gatekeepers, and temple servants, along with their wives, sons, and daughters, everyone who is able to understand and who has separated themselves from the surrounding peoples to ⌊obey⌋ the law of God—

While only the leaders signed the binding agreement, they signed on behalf of every Israelite. The mention of those who had **separated themselves from the surrounding peoples** may be interpreted in at least two ways. First, those who separated may refer to individuals who had divorced their foreign wives (Ezra 10:1-17). More likely, the separated group refers to non-Jews in the area who had separated themselves from their idolatrous ways and embraced God and His law. In any case, the binding agreement included all who had committed themselves to God.

Verse 29: **join with their noble brothers and commit themselves with a sworn oath to follow the law of God given through God's servant Moses and to carefully obey all the commands, ordinances, and statutes of the LORD our Lord.**

The Israelites who had not signed the agreement committed themselves verbally with a sworn oath. Binding agreements between kings and nations often included curses that would come upon any party that violated the agreement. Curses also formed part of covenants between Israel and God. In their prayer of confession the Israelites already had noted God's faithfulness to His covenant with Israel. By signing the agreement and taking a sworn oath, they pledged their faithfulness to God.

The Israelites promised to obey God's law as mediated through Moses. The phrase **commands, ordinances, and statutes** included all the requirements of God's law. The people promised not just to obey the major laws or the ones they found easy to obey, but to obey all God's commands.

While the Israelites committed to keeping all God's laws, their present situation demanded special obedience to specific regulations (Neh. 10:30-39). Living in an area surrounded by people of different beliefs, the Israelites pledged to forbid their children from marrying non-Israelites. They also determined to keep the Sabbath and the Sabbath Year. They promised to obey God by bringing their tithes and offerings to support the temple and its personnel. Having committed themselves to God, the Israelites committed themselves to supporting the worship of God and those who ministered.

We do not always have to publicly announce our rededication to God, but sometimes such a public announcement strengthens our commitment and creates an accountability group for us. Whether or not we rededicate ourselves publicly, we need to periodically renew our commitment to God.

FOR FURTHER STUDY

Why do you think rededication to God is sometimes necessary?

The Week of January 21
VALUING EVERY LIFE

Background Passage: Psalm 139:1-24
Lesson Passage: Psalm 139:1-16

INTRODUCTION

"That child is simply incorrigible," stated Brenda. "No teacher alive could do anything with him. Why is it that the good kids transfer to other schools while the ones we can't stand stay with us!"

"Is there no way we can get rid of Traci?" Dr. Giles asked his academic dean. "She does not try in any of her classes, she is disruptive in the dorm, and, according to many stories I have heard, does not have the morals we try to teach our students. I am sick of hearing her excuses. If she is going to stay here, and I hope she is not, I do not want her in my class ever again!"

"Just ignore him, honey," Rhonda said to her husband, Thom. "I know Glen is arrogant and hard to get along with but, even though we are neighbors, we do not have to see him and his wife socially. When he catches you outside in the yard, just make an excuse and come inside for a while. Maybe we'll get lucky and he'll move."

"Caring for Sarah has been such a burden for Sam," Ben told his Sunday School class as they mentioned prayer requests. "Alzheimer's has robbed Sarah of her life and it's robbing Sam of his life too. It seems he is just caring for the shell of someone he loved. I don't see how or why he does it."

We often tend to value people based on how cooperative or productive they are or how much they resemble us and our beliefs. When people disappoint us, anger us, or lose their ability to function and communicate, we face the temptation to see them as less than human. While we may never abuse individuals or even entertain the thought of killing anyone, we sometimes do not see people as having value equal to ours.

God values everyone because He made each person in His image. He knows each person, created each to live a special life and fulfill a purpose, and loves each one. Psalm 139 reminds us that God values each person and that we need to value each person as well.

Psalm 139:1-24
1. Unique Knowledge (Ps. 139:1-6)
2. All-Encompassing Plan (Ps. 139:7-16)
3. Perfect Guidance (Ps. 139:17-24)

THE BACKGROUND

Psalm 139 provided worshipers the opportunity to defend their inno-cence against unjust charges by appealing to God's knowledge of, presence with, plan for, and creation of them. The psalm begins by appealing to God's complete knowledge. While we may be able to hide our thoughts and deeds from others, God knows everything about us. God's knowledge can be intimidating because we cannot pretend to be what we are not. Yet, God's knowledge also allows us to appeal to Him to establish our inno-cence when we are unjustly accused (Ps. 139:1-6). God's knowledge of us also demonstrates how much He values us and desires to relate to us.

The psalm next emphasizes the impossibility of escaping God. No place exists to which we can flee from God's presence. Since nothing escapes God's watchful eye, God knows when charges brought against us have no merit. Having created us and given us a purpose for our lives, God care-fully watches us, not to punish any and every infraction of the law but to provide guidance to help us fulfill His purposes. Such personal attention causes us to marvel (139:7-16)

The psalm concludes with a statement acknowledging the impossibili-ty of understanding God's thoughts because they are infinitely beyond human understanding. The psalmist asked God to intervene and defeat the enemies who had brought the false charges. In closing the psalmist asked God to continue to examine and guide him through this experience and throughout all his life (139.17-24).

THE BIBLE PASSAGE

1. Unique Knowledge (Ps. 139:1-6)

Verse 1: LORD, **You have searched me and known me.**

The notation at the beginning of the psalm—technically called a super-scription—provides information regarding the function and authorship of the poem. The phrase "for the choir director" occurs in the superscrip-tions of other psalms (see Pss. 8; 22; 51) and probably indicates the psalm served as part of a collection of psalms used regularly in worship at the temple. The phrase translated "a Davidic psalm" is found in approximate-ly half of the psalms. It can mean "by David," "for David," or "belonging to David." Jewish and Christian tradition has long favored the translation "by David" and recognized the phrase as identifying David as the author of the psalm. David has long been recognized as a great writer of psalms or songs (2 Sam. 23:1; 2 Chron. 29:30).

Many individuals have used Psalm 139 in personal and private worship since David's time. Some Bible students suggest worshipers used the psalm to declare their innocence of an unjust charge. The use of the word "offensive" (Ps. 139:24), which also may be translated "idolatrous," has led some Bible students to believe worshipers who had been accused of idolatry came to the temple to pray the psalm and deny the charge. Worshipers would appeal to God's knowledge of them and then wait for God's vindication, perhaps through the words of a priest or prophet. The psalm does not reflect abstract theological speculation but an intimate experience with God in which a person becomes aware of God's omniscience and involvement in each life.

Long after worshipers may have recited the psalm in the temple in an attempt to establish their innocence, worshipers have continued to pray the psalm in awesome wonder at God's knowledge, power, and involvement in the life of each person. We join with those worshipers in marveling at God's majesty.

The psalm begins with the recognition God has **searched** and **known** David the psalmist. The verb translated *searched* describes a thorough examination. People searched, explored, or scouted out a land or city to determine whether they could settle in it (Judg. 18:2; 2 Sam. 10:3). Individuals searched or probed for ore in the depths of the earth (Job 28:3); investigated, examined, or searched for truth (Job 5:27; 28:27); and sounded out a person or searched to discover what he or she really thought (1 Sam. 20:12). Human searches may overlook some parts of a land, city, mine, or person. When God searches an individual, however, no part of the person escapes His knowledge.

The verb translated *known* refers to intimate, personal knowledge. The word *know* often appears in the Old Testament to describe sexual relations between a man and woman (for example, Gen. 4:1). God knows all individuals on an intimate level because He is interested in and loves each one.

FOR FURTHER STUDY

Read the article entitled "Knowledge" on pages 999-1000 of the *Holman Illustrated Bible Dictionary*. List some of the differences between God's knowledge and human knowledge.

Verse 2: **You know when I sit down and when I stand up; You understand my thoughts from far away.**

God knows everything about each person. When a person sits down to rest, eat, or worship, God knows. When a person stands to walk, work, or sing God's praises, He knows. God views our actions and sees both our obedience and disobedience.

God also knows our every thought and attitude. Sometimes our thoughts and attitudes may puzzle us. We wonder why an old memory surfaces to once again create tension between us and someone else. We wonder why we reacted as we did to a particular situation. While we may not understand our thoughts and attitudes, God does. While we may think of God as seated on His throne and far removed from us, He knows and understands who we are and why we act as we do. Time and space do not bind God. He reigns while still being present with and within us in the Person of the Holy Spirit.

Verse 3: **You observe my travels and my rest; You are aware of all my ways.**

In the Old Testament world, people believed gods only had influence over the particular nation that worshiped them. As a person traveled from one nation to another, the individual would move from the domain of one set of gods to the domain of another. Thus according to that viewpoint, when a person crossed a national border, the gods of the nation the individual had left became unaware and unconcerned regarding the location and fate of that individual.

God has no limits to His authority and knowledge. Wherever a person may travel, God knows the individual's location and cares for the individual. If the person takes up residence in another land, God knows. If the individual pauses to rest during a journey, God knows where he or she stops. In whatever way people travel or live, God knows their location and how they live their lives.

Sometimes we seek to leave one area and begin life in another place. Sometimes we may do so to leave behind haunting memories or bad decisions and begin again where no one knows what our past lives have been like. People in the new area may not know our pasts, but God does. Amazingly, God loves us anyway.

Verse 4: **Before a word is on my tongue, You know all about it, LORD.**

Not only does God hear every word we speak, He also knows what we will say before we speak. Sometimes we think of what we could say or would like to say, but remain quiet. We may congratulate ourselves on being disciplined, holding our tongues, and not hurting others with our hateful thoughts. God, however, knows what we would like to say and knows the dislike we hold for the other person. He knows how our thoughts poison our relationships.

At other times we surprise ourselves by blurting out something we had not intended to say. While we never intended to speak the words, God knows our thoughts and feelings. If we attempt to hide our true feelings by speaking in loving, friendly tones, God sees through our false attitudes. Spoken words can hurt others. Unspoken words can hurt us as we harbor hatred for others.

Verse 5: **You have encircled me; You have placed Your hand on me.**

The phrase **You have encircled me** in Hebrew reads literally "behind and before, You enclose me." As air surrounds us in our daily lives, as light surrounds us during the day and darkness during the night, so God surrounds us. He knows our movements, our locations, and our thoughts. Nothing about us can be hidden from Him.

The realization that God knows everything about us can be more frightening than comforting. We live in a time of identity theft when we do all we can to protect our personal information from falling into criminal hands. Fans stalk movie, television, music, and sports stars while paparazzi follow and study the same stars in order to get photos to sell to newspapers and magazines. Criminals study homes or businesses they plan to rob so they will know the best time to strike. Most of us protect our privacy. That God knows our every movement, word, deed, and thought could add to our paranoia.

God's knowledge, however, does not focus on knowing and tallying our every sin. God knows us because He loves us and wants to develop a personal relationship with us. By getting to know each other, husbands and wives develop deeper, stronger relationships. By getting to know their children's friends, likes, desires, and problems, parents develop deeper relationships with their children. God's knowledge reflects His desire to have a personal relationship with us so He can guide us to an abundant life in Him.

Verse 6: ⌊This⌋ **extraordinary knowledge is beyond me. It is lofty; I am unable to ⌊reach⌋ it.**

Becoming aware of God's knowledge makes us aware of our human limitations. We may believe we know our friends and relatives well, but we do not know everything about them. Their actions can surprise us. We also may think we know God fully, but our finite minds can never comprehend the infinite God. God possesses knowledge beyond what we can imagine. Like the psalmist and worshipers of long ago, we can only marvel at God's limitless knowledge and power and realize our inadequacy.

Faith does not result from an ability to comprehend God fully. Faith involves recognizing God's involvement in every facet of our lives and seeking to listen to His guidance so we may live in accordance with His will. God knows us and loves us. In faith we respond to Him.

God's knowledge of everything people do, think, or say indicates He values each person. If God did not value humans, He would not care what they did, thought, or said. God does care. He seeks those who do not know Him, sometimes by sending us to witness to His reality, forgiveness, and love. He continues to lead those who know Him to experience life more abundant.

We need to know other people as well as we can. Often the more we learn about others, the more we can empathize with them and grow to love them. Developing relationships with others helps us begin to see them as God does, provides opportunities to minister to them, and helps us value them as God does.

2. All-Encompassing Plan (Ps. 139:7-16)

***Verse 7:* Where can I go to escape Your Spirit? Where can I flee from Your presence?**

Not only does God have complete knowledge, He also is present everywhere at all moments of time. Our experience of being in only one place at one time makes God's omnipresence difficult to understand. How can God be present everywhere? The answer is that God is Spirit. While God is a personal Being, He is not limited by a body and thus not tied to a particular place at a particular time. God's omnipresence means no one can escape or hide from Him.

***Verse 8:* If I go up to heaven, You are there; if I make my bed in Sheol, You are there.**

We may try to imagine and list places where we might hide from God, but we know no such places exist. If humans try to escape to **heaven** to avoid God, they find Him there. The Israelites thought of heaven as what lay above the earth. Heaven was the sphere of the sun, moon, and stars and the rain and snow descended from heaven. From heaven God gave manna to His people to eat. God dwelled in heaven but heaven comprised such a huge place, people might have been tempted to think they could hide from God, perhaps among the stars, if only they could climb high enough. Although heaven comprised a vast place, God remained present even in the most distant corners.

Sheol referred to the place of the dead. There the dead existed in darkness. Kings had no greater existence in Sheol than did slaves. While fellowship with God was believed to be impossible in Sheol (Ps. 6:5; Isa. 38:18), He remained present.

In the Old Testament world, many people believed some gods and goddesses lived in heaven while other gods and goddesses lived in the underworld. Thus, it was thought that a person could escape heavenly deities by fleeing to the underworld or escape underworld deities by fleeing to the heavens. Since heaven lay above the earth and Sheol lay in the depths of the earth (Deut. 32:22; Amos 9:2), no place in the vertical spatial dimension provided a hiding place from God.

On Christmas Eve 1968, Frank Borman, James Lovell, and William Anders circled the moon on the Apollo 8 mission. As they circled, the crew began a television transmission to those on earth. They took turns reading from Genesis 1:1-10 and then Borman wished everyone a Merry Christmas and God's blessing. Far away from earth, they still experienced God's presence.

Verse 9: **If I live at the eastern horizon ⌊or⌋ settle at the western limits,**

The verse in Hebrew literally reads "I take up the wings of the dawn; I dwell at the end of the sea." Some Bible students suggest a reference to an ancient concept where one might magically fly to a remote location. The Israelites may have known such an idea, but the image here seems to indicate the furthest horizontal spatial dimensions of the earth.

The Israelites knew of the land of Mesopotamia and beyond. The Israelites also knew of the end of the Mediterranean Sea. When Jonah sought to flee from God's call and presence, he boarded a ship sailing to Tarshish, probably located at the southern tip of modern-day Spain (Jonah 1:3). Both journeys involved considerable danger and risk. One might imagine God's presence would not inhabit such remote lands, but even in those places, God remained present. No matter how high we climb, how deep we dig, or how far to the east, west, north, or south we travel, we cannot escape God's presence.

Verse 10: **even there Your hand will lead me; Your right hand will hold on to me.**

As the recognition of God's complete knowledge can frighten us, so also God's inescapable presence can intimidate us. We live in a time where security searches before catching a flight are common in every part of the world. Video cameras monitor our movements in buildings and on sidewalks, and cameras record vehicle traffic and infractions on the streets. Satellites have long provided detailed photos, and many of us can find satellite photos of our cities and neighborhoods on the Internet. Security may demand constant surveillance, but we still can feel uncomfortable as we have less and less privacy.

God's presence does not focus on invading our privacy. God provides His presence to enable us to experience abundant life. Like holding someone's hand while crossing an unfamiliar path in the dark or climbing stairs, so God's presence provides guidance and stability to us.

Verse 11: **If I say, "Surely the darkness will hide me, and the light around me will become night"—**

In our world we rarely experience true darkness. Streetlights, porch lights, and the glow of neon signs provide some light to illuminate at least partially the darkest night. When my older daughter took an astronomy course in her sophomore year of college, her instructor took the class out to another professor's home in the country so the students could view the planets, stars, and galaxies without the interference of artificial light. She was amazed at how much more she saw and how much brighter the elements of God's heavenly creation appeared.

In Israel in ancient times there were no streetlights, porch lights, or neon signs. Only the moon and stars provided illumination in the night. On a cloudy night, streets and paths lay in total darkness. On such nights people could easily hide from one another. People could easily believe such total darkness would also conceal a person from God's presence.

Verse 12: **even the darkness is not dark to You. The night shines like the day; darkness and light are alike to You.**

Even total darkness fails to hide a person from God's presence. Night and day are the same to God. His eyes see clearly in night or day, fog or bright sunshine, haze or clear skies. The light of His presence pierces through all obstacles.

No matter what hiding places humans may imagine, we cannot escape God's loving presence. While our bodies limit our ability to be present in multiple places at the same time, nothing limits God from being present throughout His creation at all times. We cannot understand God's ability to be present to all, but we can rejoice in His continual presence with us.

Believers uniquely experience God's presence in the Person of the indwelling Holy Spirit. However, God's presence in one sense is with all people. All people are made in God's image, and He does not want anyone to die without repenting of sin and developing a personal relationship with Him (2 Pet. 3:9). God sent His Son because He loved the world and wanted people to experience salvation (John 3:16-17). God's presence with all people, whether they believe in Him or not, demonstrates His love for them and the value He places on them.

FOR FURTHER STUDY

How can we be present with others and show we value them as humans made in God's image?

Verse 13: **For it was You who created my inward parts; You knit me together in my mother's womb.**

Long before we become aware, God knows us and is present with us. God knows us so completely because He created us. God created our human form and our **inward parts**. The phrase *inward parts* is sometimes translated "kidneys" and referred in Hebrew thought to the seat of a person's emotions and a person's understanding of morality. Along with the heart, the kidneys were believed to comprise the core of each individual's personality.

God forms each person within the **mother's womb**. God is present with the fetus in the womb. He values each child's life and has plans for each child. For most parents a pregnancy is a joyous time. They make preparations for their child, dream dreams, guard the health of mother and child, and wait expectantly for the child's birth. As parents value their unborn child, God values the unborn child even more. Each child is a unique creation of God with whom God desires a personal relationship.

Verse 14: **I will praise You, because I have been remarkably and wonderfully made. Your works are wonderful, and I know ⌊this⌋ very well.**

When we consider the complexity of the human body and the wonder of each person's personality and gifts, amazement fills us. Each of us is a marvel, a mixture of cells, organs, fluids, nerve impulses, muscles, and skin all working together to produce not just a living organism but a human being capable of imagining, thinking, solving problems, inventing, and relating to God and others. Each of us bears testimony to God as Wonderful Creator.

We all have some days when we do not feel like marvelous creations of God. Disease, disappointments, frustrations, and failures can make us feel more flawed than wonderful. The marvel of our creation does not depend on perfect health, constant success, or continuous productivity. Those who battle disease, those who struggle with making ends meet, and those who cannot function as vital parts of the economy remain valuable to God. We tend to value people based on their accomplishments. God values people because they are His creations whom He knows and loves.

Verse 15: **My bones were not hidden from You when I was made in secret, when I was formed in the depths of the earth.**

Medical advances have enabled researchers to photograph fetuses and perform corrective, life-saving surgeries on a fetus inside the mother's womb. Yet for most of us the amazing growth and development of a child in the womb remains an unseen marvel. What we see and know only in glimpses, God sees and knows in totality.

Verse 16: **Your eyes saw me when I was formless; all ⌊my⌋ days were written in Your book and planned before a single one of them began.**

After conception, a fetus seems quite formless, only a jumble of dividing cells. As time passes, specific cells with specific functions make the fetus look more like a human being with head, arms, and legs. Even though the fetus does not look human early in its development, God considers the fetus human and values the fetus. While the child is still in the womb, God has a purpose for the child that extends beyond the child's birth and throughout the child's life. God treasures the life of each child. He knows what He intends the baby to become.

God's creation of each individual to fulfill special purposes indicates the value God places on each person. As God values human beings from conception to death, so we also need to value others. We need to work with God in protecting people at all stages of life and nurturing them to accomplish their God-given purposes. We need to help pregnant mothers carry their babies to term and give their babies a chance at a full life. We need to protect children from child abuse and allow them to discover their gifts and value. We need to help young people remain free of alcohol and drugs so they can live healthy and happy lives. We need to help middle-aged adults cope with the stresses of life as parents, workers, and caretakers and offer them guidance and encouragement in making decisions. We need to respect our older adults, learn from them, and assist them as they lose physical strength and sometimes mental acuity. God has a purpose for all people at all stages of life and thus we need to value all people at all stages of life.

3. Perfect Guidance (Ps. 139:17-24)

We want to know God so we can follow Him more closely. Yet our finite minds can never fully comprehend God's nature. Our limitations prevent us from fully understanding our unlimited God who created all things, possesses complete knowledge, is in all places and at any instant of time, and possesses perfect love. Trying to understand God boggles our mind!

God's nature makes us marvel, but even more amazing is the knowledge that our great God who is beyond our comprehension remains present with us (Ps. 139:17-18). The majestic God, who created and rules the universe, provides us the gift of His continual guidance and strengthening presence.

Every generation contains individuals who focus on doing evil and bringing trouble and pain to others. David had been unjustly charged and attacked by wicked people and requested that God act to destroy the enemies. The poet declared hatred for his enemies because he believed their sin also caused God to count them as His enemies (139:19-22).

The psalmist's statement of hatred for his enemies strikes us as strange since Jesus told us to love our enemies (Matt. 5:43-44). God's patience, grace, and mercy can sometimes frustrate us as they did the poet. Despite his frustration David did not volunteer to begin a vigilante group to deal with the enemies. Instead he waited for God to act in His time.

David concluded by asking God once again to examine his entire being to determine if he had offended God in any way. The poet did not claim moral perfection but maintained innocence with regard to the unjust charge. He requested God's continual guidance through life (139:23-24). God's infinite, complete knowledge, His abiding presence, and His creation of each individual establish Him as the only perfect Guide through life. Only God can lead us to experience abundant life.

FOR FURTHER STUDY
How can we help others discover their value as special, unique creations of God?

The Week of January 28

KEEPING COMMITMENTS

Background Passage: Nehemiah 11:1–13:31
Lesson Passages: Nehemiah 13:1,4-5,8-12,15-18

INTRODUCTION

"John, remember we are repairing Mrs. Atkinson's screened porch this Saturday," Pastor Graham said as John was pulling out of the pharmacy parking lot.

"I'm not sure I can be there this Saturday, Pastor," John replied. "My wife wants to visit a garden show, and then I thought I might visit my mother in the nursing home."

"We can really use your expertise, John. Bill thinks he can install the screening, but Stan and I have no experience in this kind of repair. I was so glad you signed up for the project because you have the experience and tools we need. Mrs. Atkinson was also hoping you might strengthen her front steps. She told me she almost fell coming down them last Sunday."

"Oh, I'm sure you three can do fine without me. George at the hardware store can tell you what you need and give you a demonstration. If I get a chance, I'll try to look at her steps some time next week."

When Saturday came Pastor Graham, Bill, and Stan replaced all the screening on the porch and temporarily fixed the steps. They enjoyed working together and visiting with Mrs. Atkinson, but what should have taken just a couple of hours took them all day. No one said anything, but everyone was disappointed in John's failure to keep his commitment.

In the grand scheme of things, John's failure seems inconsequential. Yet if we cannot be faithful in small things, we will probably not be faithful in large things. Our commitment to God includes a commitment to study the Bible, to seek to know and obey God, and to support the church with our prayers, finances, time, and abilities.

The people of Nehemiah's time made commitments they failed to honor. Nehemiah called them back to obedience. His words remind us of the importance of keeping our commitments to God as well.

Nehemiah 11:1-13:31
1. Israel's Resettlement (Neh. 11:1-36)
2. Jerusalem's Restoration (Neh. 12:1-47)
3. Nehemiah's Reforms (Neh. 13:1-31)

THE BACKGROUND

To repopulate Jerusalem after the wall was completed, the people cast lots to determine who would permanently reside in the city. Of each 10 families, one was selected to live in Jerusalem. The city's inhabitants included Judeans, Benjaminites, priests, Levites, and gatekeepers who would be able to secure the city, maintain the temple, and lead worship. Other Judeans, Benjaminites, priests, and Levites lived throughout Judah (Neh. 11:1-36).

Maintaining records of priestly lineage was important for the community after the return from Babylonian exile. God had entrusted the priests with the responsibility of leading the people in worship and obedience. They needed to be recognized and held accountable. Following the completion of the wall, the community gathered for a dedication ceremony. Two processions climbed together to the top of the wall and then began to march in opposite directions. When the two groups met, they entered the temple to sing God's praises and offer sacrifices. The men in charge of the temple storerooms gathered the firstfruits and tithes into the storerooms to provide for the priests and Levites (12:1-47).

As a result of Scripture reading, the Jews excluded Ammonites and Moabites from worshiping in the temple. Nehemiah's term as governor ended, and he returned to the Persian court. During his absence Eliashib who supervised the temple storerooms allowed Tobiah, an Ammonite, to move into the temple. Nehemiah received permission to return to Jerusalem and upon arriving, quickly moved to bring the people back to obedience to God. He removed Tobiah from the temple, provided for the Levites, stopped work and trade on the Sabbath, and made the people promise to forbid their children to marry foreign wives because such women would lead God's people astray by their pagan worship (13:1-31).

THE BIBLE PASSAGE

1. Israel's Resettlement (Neh. 11:1-36)

Nehemiah had earlier noted that not enough people lived in Jerusalem to maintain and defend the city. He had begun preparation to remedy the problem by taking a census of the people in Judah (Neh. 7:1-5,73).

Nehemiah and the people decided one of every 10 families should leave their homes in the countryside and take up residence in Jerusalem. To determine who would move to Jerusalem the people cast lots. Perhaps the people threw specially marked stones to the ground and the position of the stones when they landed determined whether or not a family would live in Jerusalem. In any case, the important matter was that the people trusted God for guidance.

God can use various means to make His will known. In biblical times, He sometimes used the lot. By this means, all the people understood God had selected the families to move to Jerusalem and human favoritism had played no part. When the lots indicated a family, the family willingly moved to Jerusalem. Such a move would have been difficult as family members adjusted to a new life in a new place. Those not selected expressed their gratitude to the families who left their homes to reside in Jerusalem (11:1-2).

FOR FURTHER STUDY

Christians today do not depend on casting lots to determine God's will for His Holy Spirit indwells every believer. What are some ways God makes His will known to believers today?

The list in Nehemiah 11:3-19 somewhat parallels the list in 1 Chronicles 9:2-21. About half the names in the two lists are the same. Probably both lists drew from a list housed in the government archives. Since the tribe of Judah dominated the province of Judah, the list began with the names of the Judean family heads that moved with their families to Jerusalem. The Benjaminite family heads then were mentioned including Joel who administered Jerusalem and Judah who assisted him.

Next the list named heads of the priestly families. The phrase "capable men" (11:14) may indicate either men trained to defend the temple area or men competent for their assigned tasks. The heads of the Levites were then listed. Levites maintained the temple, collected the tithes, and led in worship. Since the Persian government had helped fund the rebuilding of the temple and the resumption of worship, the current Persian king maintained a strong interest in temple personnel and policies. Pethahiah served as the Persian king's advisor on Jewish affairs (11:24).

The Jews who did not move to Jerusalem maintained their residence in towns scattered throughout the province and beyond. Some of the cities like Beersheba lay in the Negev region, an area probably occupied and governed by Geshem and the Arabs. The Persian government allowed Jews to move freely around the empire, so Jews probably lived in a variety of towns in biblical Palestine. The list included towns in or near Judah with a sizeable Jewish population (11:25-36).

2. Jerusalem's Restoration (Neh. 12:1-47)

The list of priests and Levites who returned with Zerubbabel and Jeshua (12:1-9) expanded the list provided in Ezra 2:36-40. The priests and Levites bore the responsibility for teaching God's Word and leading in worship. Music played an important part in worship as it does in many churches today. Mattaniah and his family led praise songs.

The list of high priests (12:10-11) covered the years 538 B.C. to beyond 400 B.C. Jeshua returned with Zerubbabel and was the first high priest in Jerusalem following the exile. Joiakim probably was serving as high priest when Ezra arrived. Joiakim's son Eliashib [ih LIGH uh shib] served as high priest during Nehemiah's time in Jerusalem.

The list of the heads of the priestly families in the time of Joiakim brought the priestly genealogy closer to the time of Nehemiah. The Persians' interest in and support of Jerusalem's temple and worship probably demanded the keeping of lists of the heads of priestly and Levitical families. The Levites' leadership in worship again received emphasis with the statement that some of the Levitical families led in praise and thanksgiving, thus carrying on a responsibility assigned by David (12:24). The phrase "the man of God" describing David occurs only two other times (2 Chron. 8:14; Neh. 12:36) and always indicated David's involvement in organizing worship. Other Levites served as gatekeepers who guarded the storerooms in the temple. Worship and ministry require people serving in a variety of ways and receiving support from fellow believers (Neh. 12:12-26).

Following the completion of Jerusalem's wall, the people gathered to dedicate it. We do not know how much time elapsed between the wall's completion and its dedication. Nehemiah probably would have encouraged the people to celebrate God's blessing soon after the wall's completion. When all the people had gathered, the priests and Levites purified themselves and then purified the people. The purification probably involved fasting, abstaining from sexual relations with one's spouse, bathing, and perhaps putting on clean garments. Bible students remain unsure regarding how the priests and Levites purified the gates and wall, but agree the purification sanctified the people, the gates, and the wall for the coming dedication service (12:27-30). Such a significant moment of celebration necessitated the people's being ready to enter God's presence with praise and thanksgiving.

Nehemiah led the participants to the top of the wall and then divided the large group into two smaller groups. Ezra accompanied the group that turned south and walked along the top of the wall and Nehemiah accompanied the group that turned north. Since the wall was approximately nine feet wide, each procession had ample room (12:31-39).

The two groups met at the temple. With great joy the people offered sacrifices and sang praises to God. When the people had celebrated the completion of the temple's foundation (Ezra 3:13), those far away could hear their joyful worship. As the people celebrated the dedication of the wall, their joyful worship again could be heard far away (Neh. 12:40-43).

Immediately following the dedication, men were appointed to administer the temple storerooms. The people willingly supported the priests and Levites by giving the required tithes and firstfruits out of gratitude (12:44-47). As gratitude led to giving then, so it needs to do so today.

FOR FURTHER STUDY

How does music contribute to worship services? How can we express our appreciation and support for our musicians?

What kinds of sacrifices do people willingly make for God today? How can we encourage and support those who make sacrifices?

3. Nehemiah's Reforms (Neh. 13:1-31)

Verse 1: At that time the book of Moses was read publicly to the people. The command was found written in it that no Ammonite or Moabite should ever enter the assembly of God,

In one of the Scripture readings the people discovered Ammonites and Moabites should not be allowed in the temple to worship (Deut. 23:3-6). The Ammonites descended from Ben-Ammi and the Moabites from Moab, both sons from Lot's incestuous relationships with his daughters following the destruction of Sodom (Gen. 19:30-38). Although the Ammonites and Moabites shared a connection to Israel, tensions often erupted into warfare.

The exclusion of the Ammonites and Moabites from Israel's worship resulted from the refusal of the two nations to help the Israelites on their way to Canaan following God's deliverance of them from Egyptian slavery. Moab in particular feared the numerous Israelites would strip its land bare and consume all its food. The Moabite king Balak hired Balaam to curse the Israelites, but God caused Balaam to bless them instead (Num. 22:1–24:25; Neh. 13:2). Such fear and hatred of Israel by Ammon and Moab led to continuing conflict and distrust.

The people immediately acted to prevent Ammonites and Moabites from entering the temple to worship (Neh. 13:3). Apparently some Ammonites and Moabites lived in Jerusalem and may have been participating in worship. Those individuals could still come to worship but only if they fully embraced faith in and obedience to God and became Jews. Those who worshiped in the temple simply to make economic or political contacts or to cause trouble could no longer come. This action should not be viewed as racial exclusivism. Foreigners could always become a part of Israel by conversion (see Ruth 1:15-18).

Verse 4: Now before this, Eliashib the priest had been put in charge of the storerooms of the house of our God. He was a relative of Tobiah

Nehemiah had served as governor in Jerusalem for 12 years (445-433 B.C.), but his leave of absence from the Persian court had expired. Sometime after he arrived at the court, he requested permission to return to Jerusalem because he still had work to accomplish there. During his absence things began to unravel in Jerusalem. Eliashib, a priest, had been placed in charge of the temple storerooms. Eliashib possessed a familial and business relationship with Tobiah [toh BIGH ih], the Ammonite official who had consistently opposed Nehemiah (2:10; 6:17-19).

Verse 5: and had prepared a large room for him where they had previously stored the grain offerings, the frankincense, the articles, and the tenths of grain, new wine, and oil prescribed for the Levites, singers, and gatekeepers, along with the contributions for the priests.

Eliashib allowed Tobiah to move into one of the temple storerooms. The storerooms had been built to hold the grain offerings, incense, temple vessels, and the tithes used for worship and for the priests and Levites. In spite of the fact that Scripture prohibited Ammonites from entering the temple (Deut. 23:3-6), Eliashib had allowed an Ammonite to conduct business within the temple! Tobiah's presence in one of the storerooms defiled the entire temple. The high priest of the time also had the name Eliashib. He certainly would have known about Tobiah's presence in the temple but failed to remove Tobiah and thus participated in the other Eliashib's sin.

While most of the people may have favored Nehemiah's actions, others did not. Nehemiah's absence allowed individuals opposed to his reforms to return to their old ways. Without his governmental authority and forceful, dedicated personality, problems arose. When Nehemiah returned to Jerusalem, he quickly discovered what Eliashib had done (13:6-7).

Verse 8: I was greatly displeased and threw all of Tobiah's household possessions out of the room.

Nehemiah wasted no time in dealing with Tobiah's presence in the temple. Like Jesus cleansing the temple (Matt. 21:12-13), Nehemiah threw all of Tobiah's possessions out of the storeroom, which was intended for sacred purposes.

Some may question the wisdom of Nehemiah's action. Perhaps he could have ordered Eliashib the priest or Eliashib the high priest to remove Tobiah. Perhaps he could have given Tobiah a time limit to get out. Some situations allow gentler action; but others require stern, drastic measures. Both priests had failed to obey God. Both priests had allowed the temple to be defiled. Tobiah had consistently tried to keep the community from obeying God. Nehemiah needed to act decisively to remove Tobiah.

Verse 9: I ordered that the rooms be purified, and I had the articles of the house of God restored there, along with the grain offering and frankincense.

Tobiah's presence had defiled not just his one room but all the storerooms. Nehemiah ordered all the rooms purified. When the purification had been completed, he then ordered the proper contents restored.

Nehemiah honored God by ensuring the people used the temple only in ways that honored God. We also need to use our church facilities in ways that honor God. A church does not need to become another mall, gym, or social club. While a church may minister to people through a variety of methods, the church primarily needs to allow people to encounter God and grow in faith. As we schedule activities in our church facilities, we need to honor God by all we bring in and all we do.

FOR FURTHER STUDY

How can we decide which activities are appropriate for church facilities and which are not?

Verse 10: I also found out that because the portions for the Levites had not been given, each of the Levites and the singers performing the service had gone back to his own field.

Nehemiah discovered another problem that had developed in his absence. The people had not been giving the offerings needed to care for the Levites' needs. Since the people continued to offer animal sacrifices in worship, the priests continued to receive some meat to sustain them (see Num. 18:8-19; Deut. 18:3). The Levites received no part of the animal sacrifices and depended completely on the tithes of the people to survive (Num. 18:21). In the absence of the tithes, the Levites returned to their fields to support themselves and their families. Without the Levites to fulfill their role, worship suffered and the people grew even more lax in their faith.

Paying the taxes demanded by the Persians placed a financial burden on the Jews. Payment of tithes to the temple was an added burden. Since the people had to pay the Persian tax, they may have decided to withhold the tithe to meet their own needs. Their failure to pay the tithe caused the Levites to abandon the functions to which God had called them. Financial difficulties come upon us at times, and we have to adjust our budgets to remove extraneous expenses. As we adjust our budgets, we need to continue to support our churches and ministers. God's work needs to continue, and we need to honor our commitments to support the work of the church.

Verse 11: Therefore, I rebuked the officials, saying, "Why has the house of God been neglected?" I gathered the Levites and singers together and stationed them at their posts.

Nehemiah criticized the leaders for their failure to provide for the Levites and for their neglect of the temple. The leaders had not only jeopardized the health and well-being of the Levites, they also had disobeyed the Lord. Like Eliashib, the other leaders had failed to honor God by honoring their commitments to Him.

Before the tithes had even been gathered, Nehemiah called the Levites back to the temple and put them back to work. By failing to give the tithe,

the people had failed to honor their commitment to God. By abandoning their posts and God's service, the Levites had failed to honor their commitment to God. Honoring our commitments sometimes requires sacrifice. While God may or may not bless our sacrifice with material rewards, He always blesses us with the joy of participating in His work.

Verse 12: Then all Judah brought a tenth of the grain, new wine, and oil into the storehouses.

The people responded by bringing their tithes to the temple. The dynamic, challenging leadership of Nehemiah combined with the willingness of the Levites to serve and the prompting of God's Spirit resulted in a new spirit of giving within the people.

Giving always begins with the recognition of God's great gifts to us. The first example in the Bible of someone giving a tenth is Abraham, who gave a tenth of the spoils of victory after God enabled him to rescue his nephew Lot (Gen. 14:17-20). The legislation God gave Moses regarding the tithe followed God's delivery of His people from Egyptian slavery. The call for us to tithe follows God's gift of salvation through His Son Jesus Christ. We can never give more than God deserves. God has provided us with the blessings of family, friends, Christian fellowship, and eternal life. Realizing God's great gifts to us, we need to respond with joyful giving.

Many people find tithing difficult, yet tithing is the biblical standard and the beginning point for stewardship of possessions. Stewardship involves all of life. We need to invest our time and talents in God's service as well. Becoming fully involved in God's service brings abundant joy and blessings.

FOR FURTHER STUDY

Read the article entitled "Stewardship" on page 1534 of the *Holman Illustrated Bible Dictionary*. What guidelines would you suggest for using all we have and are to honor God?

Nehemiah established a system to ensure the tithes would continue to be collected. By selecting people with diverse roles to supervise the collection, Nehemiah hoped to guarantee all would be treated fairly. He also selected individuals known throughout the community as trustworthy (Neh. 13:13). When people trust leaders, they tend to respond with greater support.

Nehemiah then prayed that God would remember him and not erase the "good deeds" he had done for the temple and its services (13:14). The phrase "good deeds" translates a Hebrew word typically rendered "steadfast love." Nehemiah's steadfast love for God led him to commit to honor the temple as the place where God was present with His people in a special way and to provide for the needs of the temple buildings and personnel. One way we can express our steadfast love for God is by caring for our churches and by providing for our ministers.

Verse 15: At that time I saw people in Judah treading wine presses on the Sabbath. They were also bringing in stores of grain and loading ⌊them⌋ on donkeys, along with wine, grapes, and figs. All kinds of goods were being brought to Jerusalem on the Sabbath day. So I warned ⌊them⌋ against selling food on that day.

From the beginning God emphasized His gift of the Sabbath (Gen. 2:2-3) and the necessity for His people to keep the Sabbath (Ex. 31:14-17; 35:2). God had given the Sabbath as a day of rest for people to focus on Him as their Creator, Sustainer (Ex. 20:8-11), and Deliverer (Deut. 5:12-15). Only Israel among all the nations of the ancient world celebrated the Sabbath as a day of rest and worship. Thus, the Sabbath marked Israel as a special people, separated to God. Nevertheless, Nehemiah discovered that rather than refraining from typical activities on the Sabbath and worshiping God, the people continued to work.

Verse 16: The Tyrians living there were importing fish and all kinds of merchandise and selling them on the Sabbath to the people of Judah in Jerusalem.

The Phoenician city of Tyre lay on the Mediterranean Sea along the northern coast. The Tyrians had long been noted as sailors and traders who had established trade relations with nations throughout the Old Testament world. Since they did not celebrate the Sabbath, they saw nothing wrong with selling fish and other merchandise to the Jews on that day.

Some Bible students suggest the Jews believed buying from Gentiles was permissible on the Sabbath. Other scholars believe the Jews felt they had to compete with the foreign trade in order to make a living and thus felt a necessity to buy and sell on the Sabbath. By neglecting to honor the Sabbath, the people disobeyed God and ignored their religious heritage. Neglect in one area of faith and practice can lead to neglect and sin in other areas.

Verse 17: I rebuked the nobles of Judah and said to them: "What is this evil you are doing—profaning the Sabbath day?

Nehemiah rebuked the leaders for the people's neglect of the Sabbath. The leaders bore the responsibility for enforcing civic and religious laws and setting an example. Their failure indicated their own disobedience and disrespect for God's commandments. Nehemiah stated their failure to enforce the Sabbath constituted an evil act.

Verse 18: Didn't your ancestors do the same, so that our God brought all this disaster on us and on this city? And now you are rekindling ⌊His⌋ anger against Israel by profaning the Sabbath!"

Nehemiah reminded the people that failure to keep the Sabbath had been one of the sins that had led to Judah's fall and Jerusalem's destruction (see Jer. 17:27; Ezek. 20:12-24). By failing to honor the Sabbath, those who lived in the land restored to them through God's grace were again inciting His anger. If the people thought the restored walls would protect them, they were wrong. As God had punished His people's sins in the past, so He would again if the people did not obey Him.

The early church celebrated Sunday as the Lord's Day because of Jesus' resurrection on the first day of the week. As believers we need one day each week to reflect on God's goodness, worship Him with other believers, and rest from our frenzied pace. A day of rest reminds us God sustains the world and not us. A day of rest reminds us God has freed us from slavery to sin.

Honoring the Lord's Day proves difficult for some people. The needs of society require them to work on Sunday. Ministers also can have difficulty keeping Sunday as their day of rest and worship. Their concentration on helping us mature and worship often makes it difficult for them to rest and worship. While everyone needs one day each week for rest and spiritual refreshment, we need to avoid legalistically condemning those who cannot rest on Sunday (see Col. 2:16).

As each Sabbath approached, Nehemiah closed the city gates. After the Sabbath, he opened the gates to allow buying and selling. Nehemiah ordered the Levites to guard the gates each Sabbath and instructed them to purify themselves because keeping the Sabbath was a holy duty (Neh. 13:19-22).

Marriages of Jews with women of other faiths continued to be a problem. When Nehemiah returned from Persia, he again confronted Jews who had married non-Jewish women. Nehemiah rebuked the offenders and physically assaulted some of them. While his actions seem extreme, he well knew the dangers of integrating non-Jewish women into the community. Solomon had married many non-Jewish women and joined them in worshiping their gods in Jerusalem (1 Kings 11:1-13). The continued worship of other gods by Israel through the years had led to the destruction of the nation and exile. Furthermore, the people had committed themselves (Neh. 10:30) but had not honored their commitment. Even Jehoiada, one of the high priest Eliashib's sons, had married a non-Jew. Nehemiah immediately sent him away (13:23-29). Nehemiah's actions indicated the severity of the people's sin and the sin's consequences.

The Book of Nehemiah ends with a summation of Nehemiah's work. He had purified the priests and Levites, assigned them duties, and arranged for the support of worship and worship leaders (13:30-31a). As the book began with a fervent prayer by Nehemiah (1:5-11), so it ends with prayer (13:31b), a fitting conclusion to a lifetime of faithful service to God. Honoring commitments requires a faithful prayer life.

FOR FURTHER STUDY
Read the article entitled "Sabbath" on page 1426 of the *Holman Illustrated Bible Dictionary*. How can we honor God in our worship?

The Week of February 4

WHEN LIFE TURNS UPSIDE DOWN

Background Passage: Esther 1:1–2:23
Lesson Passages: Esther 2:5-10,16-17,21-23

INTRODUCTION

Antwone slowly pushed open the front door of his house and peered inside at the wreckage. What the fire had not destroyed, the smoke and water had ruined. Everything was gone: the furniture, the electronics, the clothes, the photographs, and the family Bible containing the genealogy of his family for the past two hundred years.

As Antwone stood in what was left of his living room, tears welled up in his eyes. Losing his home had been compounded by the loss of his job. Two months ago the factory had laid off workers; Antwone, as a recent hire, had been among the first to go. He had insurance that would help them rebuild, but what then? He had looked for work but found nothing. Should he uproot his family and start somewhere else? He wondered why he had experienced so much adversity in the last two months and how he could possibly continue.

Suddenly Antwone felt a hand on his shoulder. He turned and looked into the eyes of his pastor. Standing with the pastor were several members of his church.

"We are all very sorry, Antwone," said his pastor. "Since we were here last night with you, we have found and rented an apartment for your family. That truck outside is full of furniture donated by our church members. Brothers Joe and Jermale are driving over to the apartment in a few minutes where some of our other men are waiting to unload everything. Some of the ladies in the church have collected food and clothing and will be meeting your family at the apartment in half an hour. We want you to know God has not abandoned you and we will not either."

We all suffer loss and misfortune in life. Sometimes loss and tragedy can seem utterly overwhelming. We may be tempted to blame God or deny His concern for us. Yet in times of radical, unexpected change, God is our greatest help. By trusting in Him, as Esther did, we can find the strength, patience, and persistence to cope and move beyond present circumstances to a new life.

Esther 1:1-2:23

1. Ahasuerus: From King to Spurned Husband (Esth. 1:1-12)
2. Vashti: From Queen to Commoner (Esth. 1:13-22)
3. Esther: From Captive to Queen (Esth. 2:1-23)

THE BACKGROUND

Ahasuerus [uh haz yoo EHR uhs] ruled the Persian Empire from 486 to 465 B.C. During the third year of his reign, he invited Persian officials and nobles to a 180-day celebration of his power and majesty. At the end of the celebration, he held a weeklong feast for all the men in the fortress of Susa. Queen Vashti [VASH tigh] provided a separate feast for the women of the palace. On the final day of the feast Ahasuerus summoned Vashti to his banquet so he could display her beauty to the assembled men, but Vashti refused. Her refusal infuriated the king (Esth. 1:1-12).

The king consulted his advisors to determine what to do with his disobedient queen. The advisor Memucan [mih MYOO kan] stated that if Vashti remained unpunished, others, including wives across the empire, would disobey authority. He suggested punishing Vashti by removing her as queen and then seeking a new queen. Such action would serve as an example to all wives not to disobey their husbands. The king followed Memucan's advice (1:13-22).

Commissioners from each Persian province began to gather the most beautiful young girls and send them to Ahasuerus. Among the women selected was Esther [ESS tuhr], the beautiful cousin of the Jew Mordecai [MAWR duh kigh]. After a year of preparation, Esther entered the king's presence, and he selected her as his new queen. Later Mordecai learned of a plot to assassinate the king. He informed Esther, who reported it to the king on Mordecai's behalf, and the plot was foiled (2:1-23).

THE BIBLE PASSAGE

1. Ahasuerus: From King to Spurned Husband (Esth. 1:1-12)

Ahasuerus, also known by his Greek name Xerxes, succeeded his father Darius I as ruler of the Persian Empire. For approximately 20 years (486-465 B.C.) Ahasuerus ruled an empire extending from modern-day Pakistan in the east to the northern Sudan in the southwest. For administration purposes Ahasuerus divided his empire into 127 provinces (Esth. 1:1).

At the beginning of his reign, Ahasuerus faced the typical rebellions of subject peoples who were hoping to regain their freedom. Ahasuerus secured his empire by crushing rebellions in Egypt and Babylonia. Darius had rebuilt Susa [SOO suh], the capital of ancient Elam. Ahasuerus's winter residence was located in the fortress of Susa (1:2). The fortress consisted of a rectangular platform that rose 72 feet above street level. A huge wall running two and a half miles surrounded the fortress and provided protection and privacy.

After crushing rebellions in Egypt and Babylonia, Ahasuerus celebrated during the third year of his reign with a great feast. The king invited nobles and military officials to Susa to accomplish three goals. Kings in the ancient world typically used banquets to display their majesty and to maintain the loyalty of their subjects. Ahasuerus certainly intended his banquet to accomplish the same. As a third goal Ahasuerus assembled his military officers to begin planning his campaign against Greece. The banquet probably did not last 180 days, but for 180 days the king displayed evidence of his power and majesty (1:3-4).

Ahasuerus invited every male who worked in the fortress of Susa to the weeklong banquet at the end of the 180 days (1:5) . The luxury on display and the foods and wines served must have been unbelievable. The marble columns in the garden courtyard were draped with white and purple linen (the royal colors of Persia). The guests reclined on gold and silver couches surrounded by the beauty of the courtyard and the mosaic pavement. Wine flowed freely at Persian banquets, and the guests drank all they wanted from golden goblets (1:5-8).

As Ahasuerus entertained the men of the palace complex, Queen Vashti entertained the women of the palace. According to ancient historians, Amestris served as Ahasuerus's queen. Vashti, meaning "sweetheart," might have been a pet name for Amestris or it might be the Greek version of her name. Husbands typically came with their wives to Persian banquets, but men and women often separated after the drinking began. That Vashti hosted a banquet for the women indicated she possessed authority within the palace. That she hosted a banquet separate from her husband's foreshadowed the separation that would soon occur between them (1:9).

On the final day of the feast, the inebriated Ahasuerus called for Vashti to come to him so he could display her beauty to the men of the fortress. Later rabbis believed the king's command for Vashti to wear her royal crown meant he wanted her to wear nothing but her royal crown. Other Bible students suggest the king wanted Vashti to come unveiled. For a woman to uncover her face before men, especially men who had been drinking for six days, would have been a horrifying violation of custom and modesty. Vashti refused her husband's command, an action that enraged the king. Ahasuerus ruled most of the known world but could not force his wife to do his bidding. Vashti knew the possible results of her disobedience but chose to do what was right rather than what was easy. She chose propriety and dignity over shameful behavior (1:10-12).

Those in authority sometimes use power and position to demand unrighteous, immoral behavior. Taking a stand against one who can influence our career and well-being requires courage. As believers we need to act consistent with our faith in and commitment to God.

2. Vashti: From Queen to Commoner (Esth. 1:13-22)

Ahasuerus elevated a domestic problem into a matter of national concern and called upon his top advisors to provide a solution. The king had seven trusted advisors (see Ezra 7:14) who had access to him and served in top-level government positions. Advisors possessed prestige and power but also faced the wrath of the king if they provided bad advice or counsel the king did not wish to hear. Ahasuerus asked the advisors to determine what Persian law dictated be done to the disobedient queen (Esth. 1:13-15).

The fact that Memucan spoke for the advisors indicated he possessed the highest status. Memucan exaggerated the impact of Vashti's actions and claimed that unless Vashti was severely punished, women, both noble and peasant, throughout the empire would begin to despise and disobey their husbands. Memucan claimed that before the day ended the empire's social structure would crumble. Certainly Memucan's claim constituted an overreaction to Vashti's disobedience. One act of disobedience by the queen would not cause an empire-wide crumbling of societal norms and authority. Memucan wanted to provide a solution the king would like and that would keep him in the king's favor (1:16-18).

Memucan suggested Ahasuerus should issue a royal proclamation stripping Vashti of her royal title and position and begin a search for a new, worthier queen. Since Vashti possessed incredible beauty and dignity, finding a worthier queen would prove difficult. More than likely Memucan meant the king needed to find a more obedient queen. If the king followed his advice, Memucan stated, wives would honor their husbands and the empire's social structure would remain strong (1:19-20).

Ahasuerus approved Memucan's plan. He immediately sent letters to every province in the language of the province so the king's proclamation would be clearly understood. The proclamation stated husbands should be masters of their houses and should speak in the language of their own people. Some Bible students find it odd that the Persian king would encourage family heads to speak in their own native language, but the choice of language probably indicated the husband being master of his home (1:21-22).

Persian law contrasted sharply with God's law. Unlike God's law, Persian law depended on the mood of the king. If the king was happy, his subjects experienced relative peace, but if he became angry, his people suffered. In His unchanging steadfast love, God provided a law that focused on the development and maintenance of a loving, just society under His guidance and lordship. God's law reveals His compassionate nature and helps us live an abundant life.

FOR FURTHER STUDY

Read the article entitled "Law, Ten Commandments, Torah" on pages 1015-1019 of the *Holman Illustrated Bible Dictionary*. Focus on the section entitled "Old Testament." How would you compare and contrast Persian law and the laws of nations today with God's law?

3. Esther: From Captive to Queen (Esth. 2:1-23)

Some time after the delivery of the royal proclamation, Ahasuerus remembered Vashti's beauty and the relationship he had enjoyed with her. However, he had chosen to punish her disobedience by removing her as queen, and he could not change his decree (Esth. 2:1).

Memucan's suggestion had included seeking another queen (1:19). Ahasuerus's personal attendants encouraged him to begin an empire-wide search and have the most beautiful young women brought to him so he could choose his new queen. To ensure Ahasuerus would find a suitable replacement for Vashti, the attendants suggested placing the young women under the care of the king's eunuch Hegai [HEE gigh], who would provide them with the proper beauty treatments and court-etiquette lessons so the women could impress the king (2:2-3).

Unlike a modern beauty contest in which contestants can win scholarships and perhaps come to the attention of talent scouts, being selected as a potential queen held little promise of a good life. The women would never see their communities or families again and would spend the rest of their lives in the king's harem, unable to have a fulfilling marriage and children. The slim chance they might be selected to replace Vashti offered little hope. The king thought nothing of their hopes and dreams as he ordered the search for his new queen to begin (2:4).

Verse 5: A Jewish man was in the fortress of Susa named Mordecai son of Jair, son of Shimei, son of Kish, a Benjaminite.

A Jewish man named Mordecai served in the fortress of Susa. He was evidently a member of the king's court (see 2:21; 3:2). Some Bible students suggest the name Mordecai may be related to the name of the Babylonian god Marduk. Sometimes conquering nations gave captives new names to reflect their dominance over their captives (see Dan. 1:6-7). If the name is of Persian or Babylonian origin as some scholars suggest, Mordecai's parents may have given him a Jewish name to reflect his heritage and a Persian name to allow him to integrate into Persian society. Mordecai's instruction to Esther not to reveal her Jewish identity may indicate he used his non-Jewish name to conceal his own ethnic and religious identity.

Mordecai descended from the tribe of Benjamin. His father was Jair [JAY uhr], his grandfather was Shimei [SHEM ih igh (eye)], and his great grandfather was Kish. Saul, Israel's first king, also came from the tribe of Benjamin and his father also was named Kish (1 Sam. 9:3). The two men named Kish are certainly not identical because they were separated by hundreds of years, but the similar names may imply Mordecai shared a common ancestry with Saul. One of Saul's enemies had been Agag, king of the Amalekites (1 Sam. 15:7-9). Mordecai would soon face his own enemy Haman, the Agagite (Esth. 3:1). As God had helped Saul triumph over Agag, so He would help Mordecai triumph over Haman.

Verse 6: He had been taken into exile from Jerusalem with the other captives when King Nebuchadnezzar of Babylon took King Jeconiah of Judah into exile.

The phrase **taken into exile from Jerusalem** can refer to either Mordecai or Kish. Nebuchadnezzar [NEB yoo kad NEZ uhr] took King Jeconiah [JEK oh NIGH uh] (also known as Jehoiachin) and other Jews into exile in 597 B.C. If Mordecai had come into Babylonia with King Jeconiah, he would have been over 120 years old and Esther would not have been too much younger. Probably Mordecai's great grandfather Kish had gone into exile with King Jeconiah. Since those who had gone into exile with Jeconiah were members of the royal family or the upper class, Mordecai came from a family of means. His background may have helped him secure the position he had in the fortress in Susa (see 2:5,21).

Verse 7: Mordecai was the legal guardian of his cousin Hadassah (that is, Esther), because she didn't have a father or mother. The young woman had a beautiful figure and was extremely good-looking. When her father and mother died, Mordecai had adopted her as his own daughter.

Mordecai had adopted his orphaned cousin Hadassah [huh DASS uh]. Hadassah, meaning "myrtle," also had another name, Esther. Some Bible students state the name **Esther** shares a common root with the name of the goddess Ishtar, but other Bible students dispute the link. The name *Esther* appears similar to a Hebrew verb meaning "to conceal" or "to hide." It reminds us of Mordecai's decision to keep her ethnic and religious identity a secret.

Like Vashti, Esther possessed great beauty. If Ahasuerus sought a new queen worthy to replace the stunning Vashti, Esther could be the woman he would choose. As Mordecai knew and Ahasuerus would discover, Esther possessed not just great physical beauty but beauty of character as well.

Bible students have long pointed out the name of God never appears in the Book of Esther. The absence of God's name, however, does not imply the absence of His presence. Mordecai's ancestors had raised him as a faithful believer, and he had no doubt taught Esther to know and trust in God. God had given Mordecai a role that would prove invaluable and had given Esther the beauty and strength of character that would enable her to save her people.

Mordecai's and Esther's faith enabled them to cope with unavoidable changes in life. Faith in God had sustained Mordecai and his ancestors as they lived, worshiped, and followed God in an alien nation and culture. Faith in God sustained Esther through the loss of her parents. When we face unexpected change in life, our faith in God can sustain us also, helping us to cope with new circumstances and continue to follow and live for God.

FOR FURTHER STUDY
How has God helped you cope with unavoidable change in your life?

Verse 8: **When the king's command and edict became public knowledge, many young women gathered at the fortress of Susa under Hegai's care. Esther was also taken to the palace and placed under the care of Hegai, who was in charge of the women.**

The Bible does not provide the number of women brought to Susa, but several hundred women must have been selected, if not more. Those who sought the women for the king probably gave them little choice but to accept the invitation. Ahasuerus could demand anything or anyone he wished. When the commissioners found a beautiful, young, unmarried woman they believed the king might like, they simply took her. She became part of the king's harem, effectively married to him whether he took pleasure in her or not.

Among those selected was Esther. The passive verbs **taken** and **placed** indicated that, like the others, she had little choice. Hegai, the king's eunuch, supervised all the women. As a eunuch he posed no threat to the purity of the king's harem, and as a competent administrator, he had risen to supervise one of the king's most important projects.

Verse 9: **The young woman pleased him and gained his favor so that he accelerated the process of the beauty treatments and the special diet that she received. He assigned seven hand-picked female servants to her from the palace and transferred her and her servants to the harem's best quarters.**

Esther's beauty, dignity, and manner brought her to the attention of Hegai, who knew what the king wanted. Esther quickly won Hegai's **favor,** a word often used to describe God's faithful love to His people. Esther followed in the footsteps of Joseph, who had won the favor of the prison warden (Gen. 39:21), and Daniel, who won the favor of Nebuchadnezzar's chief official (Dan. 1:9). God also had destined Esther for great service to Him.

As Mordecai had cared for Esther as a good father cares for his child, so did Hegai. Hegai immediately engaged her in the year-long preparation of beauty treatments and special diet, probably putting her ahead of other women who had arrived earlier. From the harem servants, he selected seven women to attend Esther. Hegai had known the surpassing beauty and grace of Vashti and realized Esther could be the one to replace her. He acted quickly to provide the king with a new queen.

Verse 10: **Esther did not reveal her ethnic background or her birthplace, because Mordecai had ordered her not to.**

In obedience to unexplained instructions from Mordecai, Esther did not reveal her **ethnic background**. Some Bible students suggest the queen needed to be of Persian descent, and if Hegai or others knew Esther's background, she could never have become queen. Other Bible students suggest Mordecai knew anti-Semitism existed in the government. Haman's plot to kill all the Jews (Esth. 3:1-15) may have been the most drastic expression of an anti-Semitic sentiment that purveyed the court. Wishing to protect Esther and give her a future, Mordecai advised her not to reveal her background.

Once Esther entered the harem, Mordecai checked on her daily. Since people knew of Mordecai's Jewish background, some Bible students have wondered if his actions did not jeopardize Esther. Mordecai probably did not specifically ask regarding Esther's welfare, but simply inquired in general regarding events in the harem, hoping to hear news of Esther. The diverse backgrounds of the women in the harem would have helped hide Mordecai's specific interest in Esther (2:11).

For 12 months the young women prepared for their audience with the king. The year-long treatments and training probably included court etiquette and tips on how to dress for Ahasuerus as well as the beauty treatments. When the king summoned a young woman, she received permission to bring with her anything she believed might help her be selected as the new queen. If the king did not select her, she entered a second harem where she remained for life unless summoned again by Ahasuerus (2:12-14). The pressure on each young woman would have been intense and the disappointment when not selected must have been devastating.

When Esther's turn came to enter the king's presence, she asked for nothing other than what Hegai suggested. She trusted Hegai's judgment because she believed he knew what pleased Ahasuerus (2:15).

After being brought to the king's harem, Esther could have sulked or angrily denounced her fate. Instead, she continued to trust God and listen to the wise advice of others. She adjusted to her new situation and faced with courage and eagerness the challenge before her. As we face new situations and challenges, we also need to maintain faith in God and allow Him to lead us through prayer, Bible study, and the sound advice of other believers into a continued life of service.

FOR FURTHER STUDY

What guidelines would you suggest to others for maintaining a positive approach to new challenges?

Verse 16: Esther was taken to King Ahasuerus in the royal palace in the tenth month, the month Tebeth, in the seventh year of his reign.

The month of Tebeth [TEE beth] corresponded to the latter half of December and the first half of January on our calendar. The seventh year of Ahasuerus's reign would have been approximately 479 B.C. Four years had passed since Vashti's removal as queen. During that period, Ahasuerus had been actively involved in ruling and seeking to expand his empire. From 480-479 B.C. he had waged an unsuccessful war against Greece that must have disappointed him. During the cold, wet month of Tebeth, as the king grieved over his army's defeat and his loss of Vashti, Esther appeared.

Verse 17: The king loved Esther more than all the other women. She won more favor and approval from him than did any of the other virgins. He placed the royal crown on her head and made her queen in place of Vashti.

As Esther won Hegai's favor and gained the approval of all who saw her, so she won the favor and approval of Ahasuerus. He placed the queen's crown on Esther's head and formally proclaimed her queen.

After being selected as one of the young women to be brought to the king's palace, Esther actively sought to become queen. She learned the ways of the court, submitted to the beauty treatments, and closely followed Hegai's advice. She, like the others selected, probably realized becoming queen constituted the only escape from a lifetime of living as a concubine in the harem. Esther also may have believed being queen might provide her with opportunities to help her people and others. Esther met the challenges of an unavoidable change and utilized new opportunities.

Ahasuerus celebrated his selection of a new queen with a great banquet for all his officials and staff. To enable the entire empire to share his joy, Ahasuerus cancelled tax payments from his provinces and gave expensive gifts. Ahasuerus's generosity regarding his queen would be demonstrated again later when he would offer Esther even half his kingdom (5:3,6; 7:2). Finding Esther as queen marked the end of a difficult period in the king's personal life and the beginning of a promising future (2:18).

The Bible does not explain why the virgins were assembled again. Perhaps the king wanted them to appear before his new queen and recognize her status (2:19). Esther continued to obey Mordecai by keeping her ethnic, religious background secret. As she had obeyed her adoptive father in the past, she continued to do so even after becoming queen (2:20). Esther's respect for those in authority serves as a model for us.

Verse 21: During those days while Mordecai was sitting at the King's Gate, Bigthan and Teresh, two eunuchs who guarded the ⌊king's⌋ entrance, became infuriated and tried to assassinate King Ahasuerus.

One day as Mordecai served at the King's Gate, he learned of a plot by Bigthan [BIG than] and Teresh [TEE resh], two palace guards, to assassinate Ahasuerus. For some reason the two eunuchs had become furious with the king. Rather than dealing with their anger, they chose to seek vengeance by assassinating Ahasuerus.

Verse 22: When Mordecai learned of the plot, he reported it to Queen Esther, and she told the king on Mordecai's behalf.

Mordecai had access to Queen Esther and informed her of the plot. When Esther then told the king, she gave Mordecai credit for discovering the plot and saving Ahasuerus. Mordecai could have remained quiet and allowed the plot to succeed. However, Ahasuerus served as his king, and Mordecai respected those in authority as he had taught Esther to respect those in authority. Mordecai also knew the death of Ahasuerus would remove any opportunity for Esther to serve as queen, because a new king would select a new queen. In addition, Mordecai firmly believed God could use Esther to bless the Jews and others.

Verse 23: When the report was investigated and verified, both men were hanged on the gallows. This event was recorded in the court records of daily events in the king's presence.

After Ahasuerus verified the charges, Bigthan and Teresh were executed. Mordecai's service was entered into the official records of the royal court according to Persian custom. The king did not immediately reward Mordecai for saving his life. Later the king would correct his mistake and appropriately honor Mordecai (6:1-11).

Both Esther and Mordecai utilized opportunities to help others. When taken from her home to the king's harem, Esther responded positively and used the opportunity to prepare herself to become queen. When Mordecai learned of a plot to assassinate Ahasuerus, he utilized Esther's position to foil the plot and save the king's life. No matter how opportunities come to us, we need to use them to serve God and help others.

FOR FURTHER STUDY

How have you maintained God's standards in difficult situations? What guidelines do you live by for finding and utilizing opportunities to serve God and help others?

The Week of February 11

WHEN SERVICE IS RISKY

Background Passage: Esther 3:1-4:17
Lesson Passages: Esther 3:2,5-6; 4:5,8-16

INTRODUCTION

"I thought only missionaries faced risk," said Brent. "You know, people who go into countries not open to the gospel or into inner city areas. People like us who live in the suburbs and have good jobs are not supposed to face risk for our faithfulness to Christ."

"I know, Brent," responded his wife, Tiffany, "but I could not keep working in my job. I told my supervisors about some of the bad accounting practices being used, and they told me to be quiet. I had to tell the authorities, and the investigation made my life miserable. People I thought were my friends cursed me and accused me of ruining everything. I could not take it anymore."

"You did the right thing, honey, and I support you. If you want to find another job, you will find one. For now we will make adjustments. We agree we need to support Brandy through college and let Brandon know he can go to college. We will just cut back. We have done it before and we can do it again. You took an ethical stand as a Christian, and God will stand with us."

We do not have to serve in places that have high potential for physical harm or even pose a threat to our lives to experience risks for our faith. Living for Christ sometimes places us in situations where following Him requires courage and sacrifice. Such risk may not have life or death consequences, but life can become difficult, and we may be tempted not to live for God.

When the Jews faced destruction, Mordecai and Esther risked their lives to protect their people. They chose to follow God's leadership even when following brought risk. The examples of faithful obedience and courage provided by Mordecai and Esther encourage us to serve God even when risk may be involved.

Esther 3:1-4:17
1. Haman's Rise (Esth. 3:1-15)
2. Mordecai's Plea (Esth. 4:1-9)
3. Esther's Resolve (Esth. 4:10-17)

THE BACKGROUND

Ahasuerus [uh haz yoo EHR uhs] appointed Haman [HAY muhn] as his chief official. When Mordecai [MAWR duh kigh] refused to bow before Haman, Haman became furious. To avenge the insult, Haman decided to kill not just Mordecai, but all the Jews. Haman determined the month and day of the slaughter by casting lots. By hiding his true intent and offering a bribe, Haman convinced the king to allow the destruction. The royal decree that went throughout the empire doomed the Jews to death (Esth. 3:1-15).

After Mordecai learned of Haman's plan and the royal decree, he joined the Jewish population in mourning by fasting and wearing sackcloth and ashes. When Esther [ESS tuhr] learned of Mordecai's behavior, she sent clothes for him to wear rather than sackcloth. Mordecai refused the clothing, and Esther sent the eunuch Hathach [HAY thak] to discover the reason for his behavior. Mordecai reported everything to the eunuch, gave him a copy of the decree, and instructed him to ask Esther to approach the king. The eunuch returned and informed Esther (4:1-9).

Esther sent word to Mordecai that no one could enter the king's presence unless summoned by the king and she had not been summoned for 30 days. Mordecai told Esther she would not escape the consequences of the decree and suggested she had become queen precisely in order to save her people. Esther asked the Jews in Susa [SOO suh] to fast for three days in order to provide her with spiritual support. At the end of the three days, she would approach the king, even if doing so meant her death (4:10-17).

THE BIBLE PASSAGE (3)
1 - 15

1. Haman's Rise (Esth. 3:1-15)

After Esther's selection as queen of Persia and Mordecai's foiling of an assassination plot against the king, Ahasuerus promoted Haman to serve as his chief official. Haman's identification as an Agagite carried sinister implications. One of King Saul's enemies had been Agag, king of Amalek. The people of Israel had experienced tense relations with the Amalekites for centuries. Early in the Israelites' journey through the wilderness after the exodus, Amalek had attacked them, but God had granted the Israelites victory (Ex. 17:8-16). Saul's failure to kill Agag after defeating Agag's army set in motion Saul's rejection and decline as king (1 Sam. 15:1-35). Haman's identification as an Agagite recalled Israel's long history of battling enemies who had tried to destroy God's people. Haman's actions toward Mordecai and the Jews would soon confirm Haman as yet another enemy of the Jews (Esth. 3:1).

Verse 2: **The entire royal staff at the King's Gate bowed down and paid homage to Haman, because the king had commanded this to be done for him. But Mordecai would not bow down or pay homage.**

Ahasuerus commanded **the entire royal staff** to bow before Haman in recognition of his status in the court. Individuals in the Persian court typically bowed to those in higher positions, sometimes even prostrating themselves before a superior. Bowing to Haman constituted nothing unusual in that culture, but **Mordecai would not bow down or pay homage**.

The Bible does not specifically indicate why Mordecai refused to bow before Haman. Some Bible students believe Mordecai based his refusal on the first two of the Ten Commandments. God commanded the Israelites not to have any gods before Him and not to engage in idolatry by making or worshiping images (Ex. 20:2-6). Yet, the people of Israel did bow before their own kings (1 Sam. 24:8; 2 Sam. 18:28; 1 Kings 1:16), and Mordecai probably had to bow before Ahasuerus since he served the king.

Two reasons may have led to Mordecai's refusal to bow before Haman. First, Mordecai may have known of Haman's anti-Semitism either because of Haman's background as an Agagite or because Mordecai heard of Haman's animosity while serving in the court. Knowing Haman's hatred, Mordecai might have refused to bow to an enemy. Second, Haman may have viewed bowing to himself as recognition not just of his position in the royal court, but also as recognition that he possessed a semi-divine or divine status. Mordecai's refusal to bow to Haman may have been motivated by a refusal to support a claim to divinity on Haman's part.

As the only one in the court refusing to bow to Haman, Mordecai's refusal drew attention. Others in the court asked him why he refused to bow, thus disobeying a direct command of the king (Esth. 3:3). Each day they warned Mordecai and encouraged him to bow before Haman, but Mordecai resolutely refused. Finally, they informed Haman to see if Mordecai's disobedience would continue to be tolerated. Mordecai had told them he was a Jew, perhaps supposing that fact would explain his disobedience. The court officials informed Haman of Mordecai's ethnic and religious background as well (3:4).

Mordecai knew others in the court would notice his refusal to bow to Haman, yet he remained faithful to God by refusing to give honor due only to God to someone who did not deserve such respect. Knowing the potential cost, Mordecai refused to compromise but maintained his loyalty to God. We need to demonstrate the same faithfulness to God and courage in obedience even when we know such faithfulness and obedience may prove costly.

Verse 5: **When Haman saw that Mordecai was not bowing down or paying him homage, he was filled with rage.**

Haman may already have noticed Mordecai's refusal to bow on some occasions but may not have observed Mordecai's consistent refusal to bow to him. Haman's fury upon being informed of Mordecai's action indicated Haman's arrogance and pride. Haman's promotion had gone to his head and made him believe he was better than everyone else but the king. Mordecai's refusal to give Haman the recognition and reverence Haman thought he deserved crushed Haman, and he responded with rage.

Verse 6: **And when he learned of Mordecai's ethnic identity, Haman decided not to do away with Mordecai alone. He set out to destroy all of Mordecai's people, the Jews, throughout Ahasuerus' kingdom.**

Haman's action further indicated his incredible arrogance and pride. Punishing Mordecai would not be enough to compensate for the insult against Haman. Knowing Mordecai was a Jew, Haman decided to kill every Jew in the Persian Empire. This chief official believed only ethnic, religious cleansing could atone for Mordecai's sin against him.

Haman used the casting of lots to determine the day and the month on which the Jews would be slaughtered. The Hebrew word *pur* is based on a similar-sounding Babylonian word with a primary meaning of "lot" and a secondary meaning of "fate." Persians used pebbles or broken stones for casting lots. Persian astrologers typically began a new year by casting lots to determine opportune days for specific events. Haman used the casting of lots at the new year to determine the fate of the Jews and to satisfy his anger.

Ahasuerus's 12th year would have occurred 5 years after Esther became queen. The first month, Nisan, referred to mid-March through mid-April. The casting of lots determined the slaughter would occur in Adar, the 12th month, mid-February through mid-March. Thus Haman would have a year to plan the slaughter (3:7).

Having determined the date, Haman moved to secure the king's approval. Without identifying the Jews, he cleverly mixed truth with lies and painted the unnamed group as a threat to Ahasuerus's empire. The Jews were scattered throughout the empire and their laws marked them as different, causing some to be suspicious (see Dan. 6:5), but they did not defy the king's laws. The Jews had been loyal subjects and Mordecai had even saved Ahasuerus's life, but Haman knew his charges would strike fear in the king. Ahasuerus had previously crushed rebellions in Egypt and Babylonia and was in no mood to tolerate a potentially rebellious people living in pockets throughout his kingdom (Esth. 3:8).

FOR FURTHER STUDY

How do people create suspicion regarding Christianity today? What are some half-truths used to criticize believers?

To ensure the king's support Haman offered a bribe of 375 tons of silver, an incredible amount both by Persian and contemporary standards. Perhaps Haman believed he could use the plunder from the Jews to pay the amount (see 3:13). He so wanted the destruction of the Jews, he was willing to give generously to ensure their annihilation (3:9).

Haman's accusation and bribe worked as planned. Since Ahasuerus trusted Haman and feared revolt, he gave Haman the royal signet ring and granted him complete authority to act. Ahasuerus's words regarding the money may have been a polite way of accepting the bribe or a means of empowering Haman to draw on the royal treasury to carry out his plan. Ahasuerus, acting out of fear and desiring to preserve his power, condemned an entire, unidentified people to death (3:10-11).

Haman immediately set the royal scribes to work drafting copies of the order in every script and language used in the empire. Copies would go to the satraps who governed larger areas, the governors who supervised smaller areas, and the ethnic and tribal leaders who represented each ethnic group in each area. Although the Persians possessed a good communication system, several months might pass before outlying areas received the order, but no area would be forgotten (3:12).

The date when the scribes began to copy and send the order carried special significance. First, Persians believed the number 13 to be unlucky. Perhaps Haman believed the 13th day appropriate since the order was intended to bring bad luck and death to the Jews. Second, the 13th day of the 1st month was the day before the beginning of Passover. As the Jews prepared to celebrate God's deliverance of their ancestors from Egyptian slavery, the scribes were writing a decree ordering the Jews' destruction.

The order aimed for the complete annihilation of the Jews. Neither men nor women, young nor old among the Jews would escape. After destroying the Jews, the Persians would seize their possessions as an army would plunder an enemy city or nation. The slaughter would occur on the 13th day of the 12th month. The Persians had almost a year to eye greedily the Jews' possessions, and the Jews had the same period to grieve and fear their deaths (3:13).

As couriers left to carry the order to all parts of the empire, Ahasuerus and Haman sat down to a fine meal. Ahasuerus, oblivious to the injustice of the order, believed the decree would protect him and his rule. Haman rejoiced because he believed the slaughter of the Jews would finally atone for Mordecai's insult. Meanwhile, confusion gripped the inhabitants of Susa as they pondered the reason for the decree and began to suspect the loyalty of some of their fellow workers (3:14-15).

Haman turned his anger at a subordinate's failure to bow to him into a justification for genocide. Ahasuerus, who could have requested further information and investigated Haman's charges, accepted Haman's word and doomed an ethnic group to annihilation. Such actions have not been confined to the time of Ahasuerus. Throughout history pride and hatred have led to massive slaughters of ethnic groups, and the Jews have suffered more than most peoples, a recent example being the Holocaust during World War II. We do not need to turn anger over the action of specific individuals into a desire to slaughter an entire group. While seeking justice, we need to act in ways that do not destroy innocent persons or bring greater condemnation to ourselves.

FOR FURTHER STUDY
How do some people, both believers and unbelievers, display a callous attitude toward others?

2. Mordecai's Plea (Esth. 4:1-9)

Upon learning of Ahasuerus's decree instigated by Haman, Mordecai reacted with the typical expressions of great mourning and grief (4:1). Tearing one's clothes, wearing sackcloth (a coarse material made from goat or camel hair) rather than normal clothing, and placing ashes on one's head all signified intense mourning. The loss of a loved one (Gen. 37:34), the loss of a city (Ezek. 27:30-32), or the loss of one's honor and purity (2 Sam. 13:19) could lead to such displays of grief.

Mordecai walked into the middle of Susa and began to cry out loudly and bitterly. Some Bible students suggest Mordecai intended his public actions as a protest against the king's unjust decree. Most Bible students, however, believe Mordecai responded with actions appropriate to the grief he felt at the planned annihilation of his people.

By making his mourning public, Mordecai identified himself to everyone as a Jew, a victim of the coming massacre. Most who worked with him already knew his ethnic, religious background (Esth. 3:4). Any who did not, now knew and could put a face to the king's decree against the Jews. As long as people remain faceless to us, we often delay in providing assistance or protesting unjust treatment they receive. When someone we know faces a threat, we more willingly and quickly respond.

Even in his grief, Mordecai obeyed Persian law. Persian law prohibited anyone wearing sackcloth from entering the King's Gate and thus upsetting the king. Mordecai walked to the King's Gate but stopped there (4:2). If his intent had been to protest the king's decree, he might have passed through the King's Gate and demanded to see the king. Haman had told the king he wanted to destroy a group who defied the king's laws. By obeying Persian law, Mordecai proved Haman's charge to be a lie. As Jews throughout the empire learned of the decree, they joined in Mordecai's response (4:3). Their doom seemed sealed.

As queen, Esther had a number of attendants. When they saw Mordecai's public demonstration of mourning, they notified Esther. Apparently the attendants knew Esther had ties to Mordecai although they may not have known she was Jewish as well. Unaware of the decree, Esther had no idea what had brought such grief to her adoptive father. She sent clothes to Mordecai, but he refused the clothing and continued his mourning (4:4).

Verse 5: Esther summoned Hathach, one of the king's eunuchs assigned to her, and dispatched him to Mordecai to learn what he was doing and why.

Esther singled out Hathach and sent him to ask Mordecai **what he was doing and why**. Esther loved her adoptive father and wanted to help. Probably she thought some personal matter troubled Mordecai. She would soon discover that a far greater threat caused Mordecai's mourning. Esther's love for Mordecai led her to send a trusted servant so she could understand the reason for Mordecai's behavior.

Hathach met with Mordecai in front of the King's Gate. Mordecai told Hathach about the king's decree to slaughter the Jews. Mordecai knew not only about the decree but also about Haman's plotting and the exact amount of the bribe Haman had offered Ahasuerus (4:6-7).

Verse 8: Mordecai also gave him a copy of the written decree issued in Susa ordering their destruction, so that Hathach might show it to Esther, explain it to her, and instruct her to approach the king, implore his favor, and plead with him personally for her people.

Mordecai not only told Hathach about the decree, he gave Hathach a copy of it. Knowing Esther's concern for him, Mordecai wanted her to be fully informed of the threat against them and their people. Esther could listen to Hathach's report and read for herself her husband's decree.

Mordecai provided Esther a copy of the decree for more than informational purposes. He asked Hathach to explain the situation to Esther and then instruct her to approach the king and plead with him to save her people. Prior to this time Mordecai had instructed Esther to keep her Jewish identity a secret (2:10,20). At this point, however, he asked her to reveal her ethnic, religious background to the king and ask him to save her and her people. Such an act would require great courage. Mordecai hoped the complete information regarding the decree combined with Esther's love for Mordecai, her people, and God would give her the courage to act.

Verse 9: Hathach came and repeated Mordecai's response to Esther.

Hathach returned to Esther, reported Mordecai's words, gave her the copy of the decree, and passed on Mordecai's instructions to her. Esther had received complete information and a call to act. She could make an informed and courageous response.

Esther wanted to know the reason for Mordecai's actions, and Mordecai wanted her to know everything possible about Ahasuerus's decree. Knowing the facts would provide Esther with the understanding she needed regarding the threat and her need to act. We also need to gather information in order to render more effective service to God. As international missionaries learn about the culture of the people to whom they are sent and learn to speak their languages, so we need to learn about those to whom we minister. Understanding helps us match our God-given gifts to specific areas of ministry and serve God with love and humility.

FOR FURTHER STUDY
As we consider becoming involved in specific ministries, what sources might we use to understand the needs and our fitness for meeting the needs?

3. Esther's Resolve (Esth. 4:10-17)

Verse 10: **Esther spoke to Hathach and commanded him to tell Mordecai,**

Both Esther and Mordecai placed great trust in Hathach, and he did not disappoint them. He faithfully delivered their messages and, by so doing, performed a great service.

Verse 11: **"All the royal officials and the people of the royal provinces know that one law applies to every man or woman who approaches the king in the inner courtyard and who has not been summoned—⌊the⌋ death ⌊penalty⌋. Only if the king extends the golden scepter will that person live. I have not been summoned to appear before the king for the last 30 days."**

According to Persian law, if an individual approached the king without the king having summoned the person, the individual faced the death penalty. The king did not tolerate interruptions; although, in rare instances, the king might forgive an intrusion, extend his golden scepter, and welcome the individual into his presence. The law applied to all, even the queen.

Mordecai knew Persian law, but he did not know what Esther next told him. Esther stated Ahasuerus had not summoned her for a period of 30 days. Mordecai may have assumed Esther had daily access to the king. He needed to be informed of the true situation. The king's failure to summon Esther might indicate his displeasure with her. If she entered the king's presence, he might well have her executed before she had an opportunity to state her reason for coming to him.

Verse 12: **Esther's response was reported to Mordecai.**

Hathach delivered Esther's response to Mordecai. The three individuals took a great chance because some individuals in the royal court might have noticed the conversations and reported to Haman, who certainly would have been interested in any contact between Mordecai and the queen.

Verse 13: **Mordecai told ⌊the messenger⌋ to reply to Esther, "Don't think that you will escape the fate of all the Jews because you are in the king's palace.**

Mordecai warned Esther the palace would not provide refuge from the coming slaughter. He recognized the danger Esther faced if she approached the king without being summoned, but he wanted her to understand that not approaching the king constituted a greater danger.

Verse 14: **If you keep silent at this time, liberation and deliverance will come to the Jewish people from another place, but you and your father's house will be destroyed. Who knows, perhaps you have come to the kingdom for such a time as this."**

Mordecai further stated that if Esther failed to act, salvation would come from **another place**. How that might happen, Mordecai did not know, but he believed God would act.

The most well-known quotation from the book is Mordecai's statement to Esther: **"Who knows, perhaps you have come to the kingdom for such a time as this."** Mordecai believed Esther's selection as queen came not just as a result of her great beauty, dignity, and respect for the king's position and authority. Mordecai believed God had given Esther the gifts and opportunity to become queen so she could act to protect her people. Being queen provided Esther an influence available to no other Jew in the empire. Mordecai encouraged Esther to realize her God-given opportunity and responsibility and fulfill God's purpose.

Power, position, and influence are not gifts to be squandered for our own benefit. When God places us in any position of leadership, we need to allow God to direct us for the benefit of others. Only God can bring in His kingdom, but we can work with Him in caring for and encouraging others.

Mordecai had already seen God working in a wonderful way by raising Esther to be queen. Yet Mordecai also knew Esther had worked with God in becoming queen. She had obeyed Hegai's instructions and followed his advice. She had presented herself to Ahasuerus in a dignified, respectful manner. Mordecai told Esther she needed to work with God again. Like Esther, we all have been blessed by God as He has worked in our lives. He has gifted each of us with unique abilities and personalities so He can work through us to bless the lives of others and accomplish His purpose. Like Esther, we need to have the faith, courage, and love to serve God.

Verse 15: **Esther sent this reply to Mordecai:**

As a woman of faith Esther must have occasionally wondered why she had become queen. She agreed with Mordecai that her position in the royal court provided her an opportunity no other Jew had to act and save her people. She quickly responded to Mordecai.

Verse 16: **"Go and assemble all the Jews who can be found in Susa and fast for me. Don't eat or drink for three days, night and day. I and my female servants will also fast in the same way. After that, I will go to the king even if it is against the law. If I perish, I perish."**

Esther instructed Mordecai to have every Jew in the city of Susa join her in a three-day fast. Since learning of the king's order, the Jews had been fasting, but Esther called them to a more intense fast. Most fasts only lasted during the day, but Esther commanded an absolute three-day fast in which the Jews would fast day and night, neither eating nor drinking.

FOR FURTHER STUDY

Read the article entitled "Fasting" on page 560 of the *Holman Illustrated Bible Dictionary*. Have you ever practiced fasting? What is the purpose of fasting and in what situations would fasting be appropriate?

Esther's instruction to fast for her (Esth. 4:16) implied the Jews would pray for her as well. Esther intended the fast as a time to engage in earnest prayer, seeking God's help as she prepared to enter Ahasuerus's presence. Like Shadrach, Meshach, and Abednego (Dan. 3:16-18), Esther knew she might die. She asked the Jews of Susa to lift her up in their prayers, asking God to prepare the way for her so she could accomplish His purpose.

In the past Esther had dutifully obeyed Mordecai, her adoptive father. In this time of emergency she recognized the truth of his words and challenge to her and again obeyed. Mordecai then obeyed Esther's instructions to call the Jews to fasting and prayer (Esth. 4:17).

Esther willingly decided to follow God despite the risk. Yet, she did not take a foolish risk. She did not leave immediately and barge in on the king. She gathered information, listened to the advice of Mordecai, considered the need to act and the risk involved, and asked the Jews of Susa to pray with her as she prepared to approach Ahasuerus. Sometimes following God means we also accept risks, but moving too quickly ahead without gathering information, consulting spiritual advisors, and engaging in intense prayer may indicate not faith but foolishness. God calls us to follow Him. By maintaining a close, personal relationship with God, we can know the way He leads us, prepare ourselves to go, and serve Him.

FOR FURTHER STUDY

What resources can we use to maintain our faith and ethics when faced with pressure to conform to other standards?

The Week of February 18

HOW COURAGE TRIUMPHS

Background Passage: Esther 5:1–7:10
Lesson Passages: Esther 5:1-3; 7:1-6,9-10

INTRODUCTION

A father and mother take their two teenagers with them to volunteer each Saturday morning at a home for severely abused children. The teenagers sometimes miss sleeping late or being with friends, but they develop relationships with children that bless both the children and themselves. The teenagers enter adulthood with a highly developed Christian concern for others and a commitment to act to defend defenseless individuals and care for abused persons.

A physician who could make far more money in another location practices in an inner city clinic, where she often sees patients who cannot afford to pay. At the end of long days, she engages in fund-raising to keep her clinic afloat. Her commitment to poor individuals limits the college choices available to her children. One evening she asks her husband and children if they would rather she join another, more lucrative practice. They tell her no and state they could not be more proud of her work and what she has taught them.

A missionary family opens its home to sick individuals and cares for those whom the overflowing hospital cannot admit. While some family members feed and care for the patients, others run errands and pick up medications and supplies. When a patient asks the father why he took him in when no one else cared, the father responds, "The love of Christ calls me to set aside my comfort in order to care for you."

Some ministry situations require physical courage, but all ministries require us to courageously rethink and rearrange our priorities. While praying and giving money to care for downtrodden and defenseless people are wonderful, we need to involve ourselves in face-to-face ministry, working with and getting to personally know individuals who suffer. As Esther acted to save the Jews, so we need to act courageously to defend people who are in trouble or in danger of being victimized.

Esther 5:1-7:10
1. Esther Approached the King (Esth. 5:1-8)
2. Haman Plotted Mordecai's Death (Esth. 5:9-14)
3. The King Honored Mordecai (Esth. 6:1-14)
4. The King Executed Haman (Esth. 7:1-10)

THE BACKGROUND

On the third day of Esther's and the Jews' fast, Esther [ESS tuhr] dressed in her royal garments and stood in view of Ahasuerus [uh haz yoo EHR uhs]. When Ahasuerus saw Esther, he extended the golden scepter, thereby welcoming her into his presence. Ahasuerus asked Esther why she had come. Esther invited Ahasuerus to a banquet that day and asked him to bring Haman [HAY muhn] as well. At the banquet, Ahasuerus again asked Esther her purpose in coming to see him. Esther told Ahasuerus that if he approved of her and would grant her request, she would like him and Haman to come to another banquet the next day. Then she would reveal her request (Esth. 5:1-8).

Haman left the banquet feeling on top of the world, but as he passed Mordecai [MAWR duh kigh] on his way home, Mordecai refused to bow or display any fear. Arriving home, Haman called his wife and friends together, listed his wealth and accomplishments, and told them about the special banquet to which the queen had invited him. His wife and friends suggested he build a gallows and ask the king's permission to hang Mordecai. Haman immediately had workers construct the gallows (5:9-14).

That night Ahasuerus could not sleep and asked his attendants to read from the record of events in the royal court. The attendants read about Mordecai's foiling of an assassination plot, and the king realized he had failed to honor Mordecai. Haman had just arrived at the court, and Ahasuerus asked him what should be done to honor a man who had provided exceptional service to the king. Thinking the king was referring to him, Haman described what he would like done. Ahasuerus instructed Haman to immediately honor Mordecai in exactly that manner. After honoring Mordecai, Haman hurried home with his head covered in shame. His wife and friends predicted Haman would soon fall before Mordecai (6:1-14).

At the end of the second banquet, Esther revealed Haman's treachery. As Ahasuerus angrily paced in the garden, while considering how to punish Haman, Haman fell on the couch where Esther reclined and pleaded for his life. When Ahasuerus entered, he accused Haman of trying to molest Esther. Harbona [hahr BOH nuh], a royal eunuch, suggested hanging Haman on his own gallows, and Ahasuerus followed his advice (7:1-10).

THE BIBLE PASSAGE

1. Esther Approached the King (Esth. 5:1-8)

Verse 1: **On the third day, Esther dressed up in her royal clothing and stood in the inner courtyard of the palace facing it. The king was sitting on his royal throne in the royal courtroom, facing its entrance.**

On the third day of the fast Esther and the Jews of Susa had been observing, Esther put on her royal robes and prepared to approach Ahasuerus. She followed proper court etiquette by dressing appropriately. Her royal robes must have accented her God-given beauty. Esther entered the inner courtyard of the palace, where she stopped and stood in sight of Ahasuerus sitting on his throne. Esther trusted God to cause Ahasuerus to accept her intrusion.

Moses returned to Pharaoh's court after a 40-year absence to deliver Israel from Egyptian slavery. Esther returned to Ahasuerus's presence after a 30-day absence to deliver the Jews from Haman's decree. Passover celebrated God's work through Moses, and Esther entered Ahasuerus's presence during Passover season (see p. 114). God used Esther as a Moses for her time.

Verse 2: **As soon as the king saw Queen Esther standing in the courtyard, she won his approval. The king extended the golden scepter in his hand toward Esther, and she approached and touched the tip of the scepter.**

When Ahasuerus noticed Esther's presence, she won his favor even as she had when he first saw her (Esth. 2:16-17). He extended the golden scepter toward her, thereby indicating his delight at seeing her and inviting her to approach. Perhaps after 30 days of not seeing Esther, her beauty overwhelmed him as it had the first time they met. Following court etiquette, Esther approached the king and touched the tip of the golden scepter. The king's acceptance of her meant she had overcome the first obstacle to saving her people.

Verse 3: **"What is it, Queen Esther?" the king asked her. "Whatever you want, even to half the kingdom, will be given to you."**

Since Esther had come to Ahasuerus without being summoned and had jeopardized her life, he knew she wanted more than to pay a social call. Even though he had no idea regarding the reason for her visit, he knew it must be serious. Ahasuerus asked Esther what she wanted and stated he would give her **even to half the kingdom,** words reflecting the formal language of the royal court. His offer indicated he welcomed Esther and would seek to help in any way he could.

Esther had promised Mordecai she would approach the king despite the risk (4:16). Esther kept her promise. She stepped out on faith and trusted

God to preserve her life so she could save her people. Like Esther, we need to step out on faith when God calls us to do so, whether God's call is to defend others or to serve in another manner. Though our personal safety is not guaranteed, God will work through our obedience to accomplish His purposes.

FOR FURTHER STUDY

How do we prepare to step out on faith to serve God?

In the Persian Empire banquets served as acceptable occasions for negotiating and discussing important matters. Perhaps not wanting to make her plea before court officials and guards in Ahasuerus's presence, Esther invited Ahasuerus and Haman to a banquet. Apparently Esther had been confident the king would welcome her because she had already prepared the banquet. After Esther left, Ahasuerus immediately commanded his servants to bring Haman, and the two of them honored Esther's request (5:4-5).

Once Esther, Ahasuerus, and Haman had eaten the meal and wine was served, the appropriate time had come for discussing important matters. Ahasuerus again stated his favorable attitude toward Esther and again inquired about the nature of her true concern (5:6).

Esther politely answered Ahasuerus and asked him and Haman to come to another banquet the next day when she would reveal her true concern (5:7-8). Some Bible students wonder why Esther did not ask Ahasuerus for his help at the first banquet because Ahasuerus's mood might change at any time, and Esther might lose his favor. Esther followed Near Eastern custom, preparing to present her case and being content to wait for what she sensed was the precise moment to speak. Esther waited until she felt God's timing was right to present her case.

Serving God courageously does not mean acting on impulse and assuming God will provide last-minute directions. We need to prepare as well as possible so we can serve God effectively in every situation. Esther possessed a deep faith in God that, combined with her planning and courage, enabled her to defend and save her people.

2. Haman Plotted Mordecai's Death (Esth. 5:9-14)

Haman left the banquet feeling on top of the world, but as he journeyed home he passed Mordecai. Mordecai had ended the three-day fast, put on his normal clothing, and come back to his place of service at the King's Gate. As Haman passed by, Mordecai not only refused to bow before him, he refused to indicate any fear of Haman or grief concerning Haman's decree. Esther's promise to act combined with Mordecai's faith in God had removed fear from him. Haman became enraged (5:9).

When Haman arrived home, he sent for his wife Zeresh and friends to tell them about his day. He pointed out his great wealth, his large number of sons, and his high position in the royal court. He then told them about being invited by Queen Esther to a private banquet with her and the king. Furthermore, he told them he had been invited by the queen the next day as well. Life could not be better and he could not be greater, except for one gnawing problem—Mordecai. Mordecai's very presence as a living person on earth angered Haman. His pride would not allow him to tolerate Mordecai and would lead to his disastrous fall (5:10-13).

Haman's wife and friends fed his ego. They suggested he could eliminate Mordecai by building a 75-foot-high gallows and asking Ahasuerus for permission to hang Mordecai on it. The gallows probably constituted a sharpened pole upon which Mordecai's dead body would be impaled for all to see. When people saw the dead Mordecai, they would recognize Haman's great power. Since Haman and Ahasuerus enjoyed such a close relationship, surely the king would grant Haman's request. Haman loved the idea and immediately ordered the construction of the gallows (5:14).

FOR FURTHER STUDY

Read the article entitled "Gallows" on page 619 of the *Holman Illustrated Bible Dictionary*. In what ways do we sometimes create situations in which people become vulnerable or helpless?

Haman had an unrealistic view of himself and life. Arrogantly believing in his own greatness, he thought his life should be great as well. Everything should come to him, and everyone should acknowledge and respect him. The refusal of one person to bow so angered him, he conspired to annihilate a large group of people.

Life did not center on Haman nor does life center on us. Life centers on God. We have no reason to develop inflated views of ourselves nor do we have any reason to expect life will always go the way we want it. God calls us to serve Him and work with Him in fulfilling His purposes, not our selfish dreams. Working with God we recognize the worth of all people and experience true life.

3. The King Honored Mordecai (Esth. 6:1-14)

Following the first banquet with Esther and Haman, Ahasuerus could not sleep. His sleeplessness set in motion a chain of events leading to Haman's destruction. The events happened not as coincidences but as demonstrations of God's active involvement to accomplish His purposes.

Unable to sleep, Ahasuerus commanded his personal attendants to bring the royal records that chronicled the events of his reign and read from a section of the records. Undoubtedly Ahasuerus enjoyed hearing of his great deeds. They read the account of Mordecai saving the king's life by informing him of an assassination plot. After the account had been read, the king asked how Mordecai had been rewarded. The attendants replied that Mordecai had received no reward. Persian rulers typically rewarded those who had performed valuable service to them by giving them land, exemption from taxation, or monetary gifts. By recognizing individuals, kings could demonstrate their generosity and bring greater honor to themselves. Ahasuerus's failure to honor Mordecai constituted an injustice for Mordecai and a bad reflection on the king (6:1-3).

Ahasuerus immediately decided to remedy the injustice and asked which of his advisors was present. Haman had arrived at the court early because he hoped to get an early audience with Ahasuerus and receive permission to hang Mordecai on the gallows being built. Ahasuerus's attendants informed the king of Haman's presence, and the king immediately sent for him (6:4-5).

Ahasuerus asked Haman what the king should do to honor someone special. As Haman had accused a group of people of treachery without identifying them, so Ahasuerus did not tell Haman whom he planned to honor. Haman's arrogance naturally led him to think Ahasuerus planned to honor him. After all he served as the king's chief official and had only the day before attended a banquet with just the king and the queen. Ahasuerus could certainly not think more highly of anyone else in the kingdom (6:6).

Convinced Ahasuerus planned to honor him, Haman began to list everything he would want done to him so all could clearly see his power and influence and how greatly the king respected him. Haman suggested the king allow the honored individual to wear one of his robes. Wearing a robe the king had worn constituted a great honor, and some believed it actually conveyed royal power to the wearer. Haman then suggested the king allow the honored individual to ride one of the horses the king had ridden. The horse would wear a royal insignia indicating its status as one of the king's horses. Finally, Haman suggested one of the king's highest officials lead the horse around the city square and proclaim the king's special honoring of the individual (6:7-9). Clearly Haman harbored a deep desire to be king.

Haman had described the perfect way he wanted to be honored. Ahasuerus's next words immediately transformed Haman's dreams of honor into nightmares of horror and humiliation. Ahasuerus instructed Haman to honor Mordecai exactly as Haman had suggested. In naming Mordecai, Ahasuerus specifically identified him as a Jew (6:10). Haman hated Mordecai for never bowing to him and arranged to have Mordecai and every other Jew killed although he had concealed his true motive from the king. Haman had ordered the building of a gallows on which to hang Mordecai and had arrived early at the palace specifically to secure Ahasuerus's permission to kill Mordecai. However, Ahasuerus forced him to honor his mortal enemy.

Haman reluctantly honored Mordecai in every way he had suggested. Ahasuerus probably had no idea of the hatred Haman felt toward Mordecai, but many of the people did. As they watched Haman lead the king's horse on which Mordecai sat dressed in the king's robe and proclaim the king's pleasure with Mordecai, they could not believe what they were seeing. The powerful court official who openly hated Mordecai was paying public honor to him. Haman felt completely humiliated (6:11).

Haman had believed he was the one in whom the king delighted. Having to speak words honoring Mordecai brought him shame and grief. He traveled home with his head covered. In contrast, Mordecai returned to his station unfazed by the event. He did not let the honor he received go to his head. For Mordecai, nothing really had changed. His people and he still faced destruction. He still waited to see how God would intervene (6:12).

When Haman returned home, he told his wife and his friends what had occurred. After hearing about his invitation to the private banquet the day before, they had encouraged him to ask that Mordecai be hanged. After hearing of Haman's honoring Mordecai, they offered discouraging words. They told Haman that if Mordecai was Jewish, Haman could not possibly overcome him. Centuries before when Balak hired Balaam to curse Israel as the Israelites prepared to enter Canaan, Balaam could only bless Israel as God instructed him (Num. 22:1–24:25) and proclaim destruction for Amalek (Num. 24:20). As the God of Israel had defeated Amalek and its king Agag in the past (see Ex. 17:8-16; 1 Sam. 15:1-35), so God would defeat Haman the Agagite (Esth. 3:1). Haman had begun his fall, and his defeat was certain (6:13) (see p. 111).

While Haman's wife and friends discussed the turn of events with him, Ahasuerus's eunuchs arrived and rushed Haman to the banquet with the king and Esther (6:14). Haman must have trembled in fear the entire way to the palace. He must have wondered what the next few hours would bring.

Haman thought he controlled events. He believed he had engineered the destruction of Mordecai and the Jews. However, Haman dramatically discovered God controls events and works them toward accomplishing His purposes. We need to recognize God's sovereignty and our limitations. We need to serve with humility, following God and treating all persons with respect.

4. The King Executed Haman (Esth. 7:1-10)

Verse 1: **The king and Haman came to feast with Esther the queen.**

Perhaps by the time Haman arrived at the banquet, he had regained his composure. Soon, however, his past deeds would catch up with him.

Verse 2: **Once again, on the second day while drinking wine, the king asked Esther, "Queen Esther, whatever you ask will be given to you. Whatever you seek, even to half the kingdom, will be done."**

When Ahasuerus, Esther, and Haman had eaten their meal and the king was drinking wine, Ahasuerus asked Esther what she wanted. By agreeing to attend the banquet, Ahasuerus had agreed to grant Esther's request (see 5:8), but he still had no idea what she desired. Perhaps he expected her to ask for material possessions. He was ready to grant whatever she asked and indicated his favorable disposition toward her by again using the formal language of the royal court.

Verse 3: **Queen Esther answered, "If I have obtained your approval, my king, and if the king is pleased, spare my life—⌊this is⌋ my request; and ⌊spare⌋ my people—⌊this is⌋ my desire.**

Esther made her request more personal by using the second person possessive pronoun **your** and the first person possessive pronoun **my** in addition to referring to him in the third person as **the king.** While Esther was a subject of the king, she also enjoyed a personal relationship with him as his wife. Her reminder of their relationship would make her revelation to the king all the more horrifying to him.

Esther then asked Ahasuerus to spare her life and the lives of her people. Although Esther stated two separate requests, both comprised one plea. She identified herself as part of a group marked for destruction.

Verse 4: **For my people and I have been sold out to destruction, death, and extermination. If we had merely been sold as male and female slaves, I would have kept silent. Indeed, the trouble wouldn't be worth burdening the king."**

Esther told Ahasuerus she and her people had **been sold out**. The phrase *sold out* sometimes indicated being handed over or betrayed and implied treachery. Esther then used words that call to mind Haman's decree (see 3:13), as she informed Ahasuerus that she and her people had been marked for **destruction, death, and extermination.** Ahasuerus had given his royal signet ring to Haman to authorize the slaughter. Since he had not inquired regarding the identity of the marked group, he may have forgotten about the decree. If he remembered it, he certainly had no idea the order threatened Esther.

Ahasuerus's failure to gather information regarding the identity of the people Haman wanted to slaughter and investigate the charges placed guilt on him, but Esther carefully worded her statement to excuse the king. By using the passive voice *(have been sold)*, she placed the blame on someone other than Ahasuerus.

Esther then stated that if she and her people had been simply marked to be sold as slaves, she would never have bothered the king. As slaves Esther and her people could still have served the king, but if she and her people were exterminated, the king would suffer great loss. The bribe of 375 tons of silver that Haman had offered the king (3:9) seemed an enormous sum, but the loss of a substantial group of people either as workers or taxpayers would cost the king a greater sum over time.

Ahasuerus may have forgotten the decree, but Haman had not. We can only imagine the thoughts racing through Haman's mind as Esther presented her request and referred to the decree he had written. Haman had never dreamed Esther was a Jew! He had not imagined his death decree would mark the queen for slaughter!

Verse 5: King Ahasuerus spoke up and asked Queen Esther, "Who is this, and where is the one who would devise such a scheme?"

Horrified, Ahasuerus asked the identity of the one who dared to jeopardize the life of his queen. Esther rested in Ahasuerus's favor. Anyone who dared to kill her would face his wrath.

Verse 6: Esther answered, "The adversary and enemy is this evil Haman." Haman stood terrified before the king and queen.

Esther identified Haman as the enemy. She realized she presented Ahasuerus with a difficult choice. The king could believe her, his beautiful, favored queen, or Haman, his trusted advisor. Ahasuerus remembered Haman's charges against an unidentified people and his request to destroy them. He had not realized then that the order placed his queen in danger. Like Mordecai, Esther had helped him foil an enemy's plot.

Complete terror gripped Haman as he stood before Ahasuerus and Esther. His evil had been exposed and his fate seemed certain.

Esther provided Ahasuerus not just with Haman's name but also with all the information Ahasuerus needed to understand the situation and act. When we seek to defend individuals or groups, we also need to do the required research and then plan how to present the information to those who can help. By speaking the truth clearly and compassionately, we can work with God in helping those in authority to help people in need.

Ahasuerus typically turned to his advisors for advice, but Haman, his most trusted advisor, had proven to be his enemy. Not knowing what to do and confused by the turn of events, Ahasuerus left the room where he had dined with Esther and Haman and retreated to the palace garden to think and calm down. Haman, knowing he faced the wrath of Ahasuerus, remained behind to plead with Esther to spare his life (7:7).

As Esther reclined on her couch, Haman fell down on the couch pleading for his life. He probably grabbed her feet and kissed them. Haman had first become angry when the Jew Mordecai refused to bow before him (3:5). Yet Haman bowed before the Jew Esther in hopes of escaping death (7:8).

Ahasuerus then reentered the room and accused Haman of assaulting his wife. In the ancient world, kings viewed a man who made sexual advances to the queen as traitors who were trying to steal the throne (see 2 Sam. 16:21-22). Haman did not intend a physical or sexual assault, but Ahasuerus, already furious with him, saw Haman's action as the last straw.

As soon as Ahasuerus had spoken, "Haman's face was covered" (Esth. 7:8). Based on Greek and Roman texts some Bible students suggest a condemned criminal's face was covered, but no evidence exists that Persians practiced the custom. Haman had earlier covered his own head in shame when he came home after being forced to honor Mordecai (6:12). Perhaps Haman again covered his head or perhaps the words mark him as guilty.

Verse 9: Harbona, one of the royal eunuchs, said: "There is a gallows 75 feet tall at Haman's house that he made for Mordecai, who ⌊gave⌋ the report that saved the king." The king commanded, "Hang him on it."

Harbona, one of Ahasuerus's royal eunuchs (1:10), suggested a fitting punishment for Haman and provided another reason he deserved the death penalty. Harbona noted the gallows on which Haman planned to hang Mordecai who had **saved the king**. Ahasuerus immediately condemned Haman to be hung on the gallows he had built.

Verse 10: They hanged Haman on the gallows he had prepared for Mordecai. Then the king's anger subsided.

Biblical proverbs support what happened to Haman. Those who plan the destruction of others often fall prey to their own plans (Prov. 26:27). The wicked will fail and the righteous will witness their fall (29:16). Haman's arrogance and pride caused his downfall (16:18).

Esther risked her life to save her people. While God preserved the lives of Esther and Mordecai, other believers throughout history have died attempting to defend others. While God does not guarantee our physical safety, He guarantees His presence with us to give us courage, wisdom, and compassion. Believers also have the certainty of life with Him after death. Acting may bring only partial success, but not acting brings total failure. We need to do all we can to defend helpless and vulnerable people, as we trust God to use us to help them.

FOR FURTHER STUDY

What individuals in your community need someone to defend them? How are you and your church ministering to their needs or what can you do to minister to their needs?

The Week of February 25

WHAT IS WORTH CELEBRATING

Background Passage: Esther 8:1–10:3
Lesson Passages: Esther 8:3,6-8,11; 9:1-2,20-22

INTRODUCTION

Don sat with his wife, Julie, in their den, staring contentedly into the fire.

"We have done very well, Julie. A nice home all paid for. Both children through college. Now they have good jobs, great spouses, and wonderful children. Our health has been good, and we are moving toward retirement well off financially. I'd say we have done quite well for ourselves."

"I think you are forgetting Someone," responded Julie.

"True, I am forgetting several someones. My parents and yours certainly provided wonderful guidance for us and helped us financially in our early years together. We also have supportive friends."

"No, I was thinking about God," answered Julie. "He has been a constant, guiding presence in our lives. He has blessed us with a fine family, wonderful friends, a warm church fellowship, and satisfaction in life. He has been with us through the rough times like your father's decline because of Alzheimer's and my surgery. God has also helped us to enjoy and appreciate our blessings. Because of God's presence, we have a wonderful quality of life."

"You're right, Julie. Sometimes I think only of what we have done without thinking of what God has done for us. Thanks for reminding me."

Like Don, we sometimes forget God's blessings and thus do not celebrate His involvement in our lives. Perhaps our gratefulness for salvation has lessened with the passage of time. Perhaps we have not recognized God's involvement recently in our lives. Esther and Mordecai encouraged the Jews to recognize and celebrate God's saving them from Haman's decree. We also need to celebrate God's mighty acts on our behalf.

Esther 8:1–10:3
1. King Ahasuerus's Second Edict (Esth. 8:1-17)
2. Jews' Victories and Celebration (Esth. 9:1-32)
3. Mordecai's Vindication (Esth. 10:1-3)

THE BACKGROUND

Ahasuerus [uh haz yoo EHR uhs] gave Esther [ESS tuhr] Haman's [HAY muhns] estate and promoted Mordecai [MAWR duh kigh] to Haman's former position. Since Haman's decree remained in effect, Esther begged Ahasuerus to revoke Haman's order. Ahasuerus reminded Esther a decree written and sealed with the king's signet ring could not be revoked, but he empowered Esther to write what she wanted to save the Jews and affix his seal to it. Mordecai wrote a decree allowing Jews to assemble and defend themselves against their enemies on the exact day, the 13th of Adar [AY dahr], Haman had determined to annihilate the Jews. Mordecai sent the decree throughout the Persian Empire causing the Jews and others to rejoice (Esth. 8:1-17).

When the 13th day of Adar arrived, the Jews destroyed their enemies, including Haman's 10 sons, but did not keep their enemies' possessions for themselves. When Ahasuerus received the news of the loss in Susa, he asked what else Esther desired. Esther asked for an additional day for the Jews in Susa to deal with their remaining enemies. Ahasuerus granted her request. Mordecai wrote a summary of all the events that had occurred and sent a copy to all the Jews so they would understand what God had done and why they needed to celebrate Purim. Esther wrote and sent a second letter confirming Mordecai's words (9:1-32).

Ahasuerus imposed a tax across his vast empire. Persian records detailed his accomplishments and those of Mordecai. Mordecai served Persia as second only to Ahasuerus and worked tirelessly for the welfare of the Jews (10:1-3).

THE BIBLE PASSAGE

1. King Ahasuerus's Second Edict (Esth. 8:1-17)

Typically in the Persian Empire, the state seized the estate of a traitor or condemned criminal. Haman must have possessed great riches, so his estate would have been quite valuable. His estate probably included his property, possessions, servants, and perhaps even his family. In a generous gesture Ahasuerus gave Haman's estate to his beloved queen (8:1). The intended victim inherited the wealth of the criminal.

After Ahasuerus had dealt with the traitor, he turned to honor the one who had earlier saved his life and who Ahasuerus learned served as Esther's guardian. Ahasuerus elevated Mordecai to Haman's former position and gave Mordecai the signet ring Haman had worn. The ring indicated power and trust. Haman's lust for power had rendered him untrustworthy. Knowing Mordecai's character, Ahasuerus knew he could trust him with power and responsibility. Esther then placed Mordecai in charge of Haman's estate (8:2). Everything Haman had possessed passed to Mordecai.

Verse 3: **Then Esther addressed the king again. She fell at his feet, wept, and begged him to revoke the evil of Haman the Agagite, and his plot he had devised against the Jews.**

While Ahasuerus had executed the Jews' enemy Haman and rewarded Esther and Mordecai, Haman's decree remained in effect. The Jews still faced annihilation. Saving Esther had been Ahasuerus's chief concern. He may have forgotten the threat still facing Esther's people, but Esther had not. She fell weeping at Ahasuerus's feet and begged him to revoke Haman's decree. She could not be content with her own deliverance when her people still faced death. Only when the Jews were out of danger would justice be served.

As Ahasuerus had before (see 5:2), he extended his royal scepter toward Esther, thus indicating his favor and allowing her to approach and make her request (8:4). Esther used great diplomacy in appealing to Ahasuerus's best interests and to his love for her. She suggested saving the Jews would both please the king and be a just action, something his subjects would respect. She also reminded her husband of his appreciation for her beauty and his love for her. In making her request, she used the term "documents" to refer to Haman's order rather than "law," because she knew a Persian law could not be revoked. In addition, she blamed Haman alone for jeopardizing the Jews, absolving Ahasuerus (8:5).

Verse 6: **For how could I bear to see the evil that would come on my people? How could I bear to see the destruction of my relatives?"**

Finally, Esther appealed to her identity as a Jew. While Ahasuerus had saved her and Mordecai, the annihilation of her people would destroy her. Esther asked Ahasuerus to demonstrate his love for her by acting to preserve her people.

Verse 7: **King Ahasuerus said to Esther the Queen and to Mordecai the Jew, "Look, I have given Haman's estate to Esther, and he was hanged on the gallows because he attacked the Jews.**

Ahasuerus reminded Esther that he had already executed Haman for endangering her and given her Haman's estate. The king probably believed he had done enough, yet his response also indicated he was favorably disposed toward Esther. Having protected her and given her Haman's estate, he would allow her to act as she saw fit.

Verse 8: **You may write in the king's name whatever pleases you concerning the Jews, and seal it with the royal signet ring. A document written in the king's name and sealed with the royal signet ring cannot be revoked."**

Ahasuerus gave Esther freedom to deal with the problem in any way she desired. Earlier Ahasuerus had offered his wife whatever she wanted, even half his kingdom (5:3,6). He authorized Esther and Mordecai to write whatever they wished to save their people and then seal it with the royal signet ring he had given Mordecai. The king's response far exceeded Esther's request. She hoped for a simple revoking of Haman's decree, but Ahasuerus gave her great authority in the matter. Whatever she ordered would be done; but he warned her that once written, a Persian law could not be revoked.

Approximately 70 days following the writing of Haman's decree (see 3:12), Mordecai summoned the royal scribes to write his decree. Mordecai intended to send the edict to every satrap, governor, and official in Persia's 127 provinces. As Haman had instructed the scribes to write his decree in every language (3:12), Mordecai ordered the same, emphasizing the use of the Jewish script and language for the copies sent to them. When the scribes had completed the copying, Mordecai sealed each document with the royal signet ring and sent the documents by couriers riding the king's fastest horses (8:9-10). Knowing Jews throughout the empire were mourning their fate and their enemies were counting the days until they could attack and plunder the Jews, Mordecai wanted the edict delivered as soon as possible to bring hope to the Jews and instill fear in their enemies.

Verse 11: The king's edict gave the Jews in each and every city the right to assemble and defend themselves, to destroy, kill, and annihilate every ethnic and provincial army hostile to them, including women and children, and to take their possessions as spoils of war.

Mordecai's decree gave Jews across the empire the right to assemble and defend themselves from any enemy. Using the same words as those in Haman's decree (3:13), the Jews had permission to **destroy, kill, and annihilate** any enemy, including women and children, that attacked and take their enemies' possessions for themselves as spoils of war. Mordecai's decree, however, set limits to the Jews' actions.

Mordecai's decree confined the Jews' right to defend themselves to one day, the 13th day of Adar, the exact day Haman had determined to exterminate the Jews (3:13). Mordecai nullified Haman's decree by empowering the Jews to defend themselves on the day Haman had chosen to annihilate them (8:12). Those who intended harm to the Jews would think twice before striking.

Esther and Mordecai sought a just solution within the Persian legal system. Mordecai carefully wrote an edict that would nullify Haman's and save the Jews. Neither Esther nor Mordecai used the law for personal, ethnic, or religious advantage. They strove to use the law to bring life rather than death. Christians in democratic societies have responsibility not only for obeying laws but also for doing what they can to influence just and equitable legislation. We need to support legislation that demonstrates God's care for all people.

FOR FURTHER STUDY

How have believers in the past worked to provide justice for all people? How can believers today work through legal means to provide justice and life to those who suffer oppression?

Couriers delivered copies of the decree to every province of the empire (8:13-14). Everyone needed to know. The Jews needed to know so they could rejoice at God's deliverance and prepare to meet any threat. Non-Jews needed to know so they could abandon plans to destroy and loot.

Mordecai left the palace clothed in garments appropriate to his new position. After receiving Haman's decree, the citizens of Susa had experienced confusion (3:15). Mordecai may well have been popular and Haman's decree may have upset many in Susa. Mordecai's promotion and the new decree brought joy. Throughout the empire Jews rejoiced in their deliverance. God had turned their mourning and fasting (see 4:3) into ecstatic joy! Mordecai's edict also made many non-Jewish individuals claim to be Jewish out of fear (8:15-17). They wanted to preserve their lives by joining with the favored Jews. While most of these people did not convert to Judaism, perhaps some eventually came to know the God of the Jews and followed Him in faith.

God worked to preserve His people by softening Ahasuerus's heart and allowing Mordecai to write a new edict that permitted the Jews to defend themselves. National laws may not always protect us as believers, but God's presence remains with us in all circumstances and impels us to seek to protect others through just and equitable laws.

FOR FURTHER STUDY

What legitimate means do believers have today to defeat those who would harm them? How might believers employ those means?

2. Jews' Victories and Celebration (Esth. 9:1-32)

Verse 1: The king's command and law went into effect on the thirteenth day of the twelfth month, the month Adar. On the day when the Jews' enemies had hoped to overpower them, just the opposite happened. The Jews overpowered those who hated them.

Eleven months had passed since Haman's decree (3:12) and almost nine months since Mordecai composed and circulated his edict (8:9). The two conflicting edicts must have caused confusion and speculation throughout the empire as people waited to see what would happen. Those committed to slaughtering the Jews may have waited expectantly for the 13th day of Adar to enact Haman's decree (see 3:13). Instead, when the 13th of Adar arrived, the Jews overpowered their enemies. As God turned Balaam's planned cursing of Israel into a blessing (Deut. 23:5), so He turned a day of defeat into a day of victory for the Jews.

Throughout Esther's life, God had turned the tables. Haman desired honor (Esth. 3:5), but his enemy Mordecai received honor (6:11; 8:15-16). Haman plotted to kill Mordecai (5:14) but was executed and his body displayed on the very gallows he had constructed to hang Mordecai (7:10). In a final reversal, the Jews, marked for death, experienced victory and deliverance.

Verse 2: In each of King Ahasuerus' provinces the Jews assembled in their cities to attack those who intended to harm them. Not a single person could withstand them; terror of them fell on every nationality.

The Jews had ample time to prepare for the 13th of Adar. When the day came, they acted, legally assembling throughout the empire to attack their enemies (8:11). The phrase **to attack** translates the Hebrew phrase "to send a hand against." The phrase is used elsewhere in the Book of Esther to describe the eunuchs' plan to assassinate Ahasuerus (2:21; 6:2) and Haman's desire not just to do away with Mordecai but to destroy all the Jews (3:6). The phrase **those who intended to harm them** translates the Hebrew phrase "seekers of their evil," a phrase used to describe individuals who sought to destroy others (Ps. 71:13,24). Though Haman had died, the Jews faced additional enemies who desired to annihilate them.

The statement **not a single person could withstand them** does not imply no one attacked the Jews, but rather no one could prevail against them. The Jews had received legal permission to deal with their enemies, and they had used their time wisely in preparation.

Throughout history believers have faced times of persecution with no legal recourse. At other times believers have enjoyed at least some legal protection. When legal protection exists, God helps believers take advantage of the available legitimate means to protect themselves and defeat their persecutors. We can rely on the Lord to help His people take advantage of legitimate means of defeating those who would harm them.

As the 13th of Adar approached, power in Persia clearly shifted from Haman and his followers to Mordecai and the Jews. Haman's edict promised royal troops to help in the slaughter of the Jews, but Mordecai's rise to Haman's position and his edict made royal help improbable. Mordecai had become a powerful person in Persia. As his fame and authority became known in the time leading up to the 13th of Adar, support for the Jews grew and royal officials became reluctant to enforce Haman's decree (Esth. 9:3-4).

On the 13th of Adar the Jews destroyed their enemies. Some groups, like professional soldiers loyal to Haman and individuals who shared Haman's hatred for the Jews and hoped to profit from the plunder, probably attacked the Jews. The Jews also conducted preemptive strikes against their enemies to defend themselves. The Jews knew the identity of their enemies because after Haman's decree, they had revealed themselves and prepared to kill the Jews in their areas. Their commitment to the destruction of the Jews would not diminish, and thus they provided a continuing threat. Mordecai's edict authorized the Jews to defend themselves against all who attacked them or sought to destroy them. The Jews acted legally to defend themselves by removing their enemies (9:5).

While most in Susa supported the Jews (8:15), some did not. The Jews killed 500 enemies in Susa, a significant group, but not a high percentage of the city's population. Among the 500 killed were Haman's 10 sons. They had lost their father and their inheritance. They would remain enemies of the Jews as long as they lived and continue their father's ways. With the death of Haman the Agagite's [AY gag ights] sons, his line came to an end, and Saul's failure to destroy King Agag and the Amalekites was rectified (9:6-10a).

In war, the victor took the spoils. When the people of Israel entered Canaan and engaged in holy war, they were commanded to kill the inhabitants, burn all that could be burned, and place gold and silver in the tabernacle treasury because God would fight for them and they were not to profit from God's victory. The Jews in Persia also recognized God brought them victory, and they refused to take the spoils that belonged to Him. The Jews fought for justice, not to enrich themselves (9:10b). Their action stands in direct contrast to that of Saul, who disobeyed the Lord by taking plunder from the Amalekites (1 Sam. 15:17-23).

Ahasuerus learned the death toll in Susa and reported it to Esther. The king also prepared to give Esther whatever else she wanted (9:11-12). Esther made two further requests of her husband. First, she asked permission to allow the Jews in Susa an extra day to deal with their remaining enemies. Second, Esther asked permission to hang the bodies of Haman's sons to indicate their humiliation and disgrace. Ahasuerus granted permission (9:13-15).

Outside Susa the Jews killed 75,000 enemies, a number that reflects God's great victory. As in Susa, the Jews throughout the empire did not seize the plunder. After their God-given victory, the Jews feasted and rejoiced on the 14th of Adar, celebrating the rest God had provided (9:16-17).

Purim [PYOO rim] originated as a celebration of God's victory over the Jews' enemies. Since the Jews in Susa fought for two days, they celebrated on the 15th of Adar, while the Jews outside Susa rested and celebrated on the 14th of Adar. With Esther as queen, Mordecai as Ahasuerus's top official, and their enemies dead, the Jews could enjoy a peaceful time of rejoicing, feasting, and gift-giving (9:18-19). Giving gifts constitutes a wonderful way to celebrate a sacred event and share with others the generosity we have received from God.

Verse 20: Mordecai recorded these events and sent letters to all the Jews in all of King Ahasuerus' provinces, both near and far.

Mordecai summarized the events from Haman's initial hatred of him and edict to destroy the Jews to Mordecai's edict and the Jews' victory over their enemies. Mordecai then sent copies of his summary to every Jewish community in the Persian Empire so all Jews would know what God had accomplished.

FOR FURTHER STUDY

Why is it important to record history? How can written history strengthen our faith?

Verse 21: ⌊He ordered⌋ them to celebrate the fourteenth and fifteenth days of the month Adar every year

Mordecai's letter intended not just to inform the Jews regarding the events of the past year but also to establish a permanent, annual celebration. Mordecai instructed Jews throughout the empire to celebrate both days in commemoration of the victory God had given.

Verse 22: because during those days the Jews got rid of their enemies. That was the month when their sorrow was turned into rejoicing and their mourning into a holiday. They were to be days of feasting, rejoicing, and of sending gifts to one another and the poor.

Purim celebrated the great reversal God had accomplished. The Jews marked for destruction triumphed instead over their enemies. God turned sorrow and mourning into unrestrained joy and celebration. God had saved His people by delivering them from their enemies even in exile. To celebrate the Jews gave gifts to one another emphasizing their community as a people of faith.

Celebrations help us remember what God has done for us. Mordecai wanted the Jews of his generation and those to come to remember and celebrate God's goodness, so he instituted a permanent celebration. As believers we need to celebrate on a regular basis what God has done for us as individuals, in our local churches, and in His world. Regular celebrations help us retain a sharp and vivid memory of God's gracious acts.

The Jews made the 14th and 15th of Adar an annual religious celebration. The celebration received the name *Purim* from the Hebrew word *pur* based on the Babylonian word meaning "lot" (9:23-26a). Haman used the lot to determine when to annihilate the Jews. The Jews named the celebration Purim, the plural form of *pur,* as a reminder of how God had changed their fate and brought victory. The plural may refer to the two days of the celebration or to the two fates of the Jews; namely that Haman plotted death, but God decreed life.

FOR FURTHER STUDY
Read the article "Festivals" on pages 567-573 of the *Holman Illustrated Bible Dictionary*, paying special attention to the Jewish calendar on pages 570-571 and to the discussion of Purim. What annual celebrations remind us of God's blessings? What celebrations would you like to add?

The brief summary of events (9:24-26a) omits the role of Esther and Mordecai in saving the Jews. Instead, Ahasuerus became the hero who reversed Haman's plan and executed him.

The Jews of Mordecai's time and since have celebrated Purim in remembrance of God's victory in Esther's time (9:26b-32). Typically Purim occurs in March with the day before Purim being the Fast of Esther. On Purim Jews gather for the reading of the Book of Esther. The celebration includes feasting, joy, and gift-giving.

We all need opportunities to celebrate the goodness of life and God's blessings. As believers we can joyously celebrate God's provision of salvation at Christmas and Easter, but we also need to find other ways to celebrate God's gracious acts in our own lives and churches.

3. Mordecai's Vindication (Esth. 10:1-3)

The end of the Book of Esther returns us to the beginning by emphasizing Ahasuerus's vast empire and wealth. The book began with the king demonstrating his greatness by giving lavish banquets (1:3-9; 2:18). The book ends with Ahasuerus maintaining his great wealth and power (10:1).

As Ahasuerus's second in command, Mordecai participated in his greatness and entered the historical records of the Persian Empire. Yet, Mordecai did not employ his power for selfish reasons. He used his position and influence to work for the good of the Jews (10:2-3). No doubt Esther did the same as queen. Through these two faithful individuals, God worked to deliver His people and bring them peace and security.

Mordecai's vindication indicates God's commitment to and involvement with His people. God continues to act in our world today. His activity has blessed and sustained us and given us hope and direction. Let us remember His works and celebrate.

FOR FURTHER STUDY
How can we remember and celebrate God's activity in difficult times?